Still at the Cottage

Also by Charles Gordon

The Grim Pig
At the Cottage
How to Be Not Too Bad
The Canada Trip
The Governor General's Bunny Hop

Still at the Cottage

Charles Gordon

With Illustrations by
Graham Pilsworth

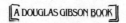

McCLELLAND & STEWART

Library and Archives Canada Cataloguing in Publication

Gordon, Charles, 1940–
Still at the Cottage / Charles Gordon.

ISBN 13: 978-0-7710-3414-5
ISBN 10: 0-7710-3414-8

1. Vacation homes – Humour. 2. Canadian wit and humour (English).
I. Title.

PN6231.C65G67 2006   C818'.5402   C2005-907318-7

We acknowledge the financial support of the Government of Canada
through the Book Publishing Industry Development Program and
that of the Government of Ontario through the Ontario Media
Development Corporation's Ontario Book Initiative. We further
acknowledge the support of the Canada Council for the Arts and the
Ontario Arts Council for our publishing program.

Typeset in Janson by M&S, Toronto
Printed and bound in Canada

A Douglas Gibson Book

This book is printed on acid-free paper that is 100% recycled,
ancient-forest friendly (100% post-consumer recycled).

McClelland & Stewart Ltd.
75 Sherbourne Street
Toronto, Ontario
M5A 2P9
www.mcclelland.com

1 2 3 4 5   10 09 08 07 06

Contents

For John, the only guy I don't mind losing to.

Introduction

At the Cottage, the work that this book attempts to update, was published in 1989. Cottages were not exactly new then; what was new was that anyone would consider them worth writing about.

The cottage, whether it was called a cottage or a camp or a cabin or a summer place, was pretty much taken for granted by Canadians. Some people had them and some people didn't. The people who had them thought about them in a practical way – did the dock need fixing, did the mice get in over the winter, were the taxes going up, how bad did the outhouse smell? The people who didn't have cottages didn't think about them all that much; they were places other people went because they inherited them from their grandfathers.

A lot has changed in seventeen years. The cottage has become an industry, something the expression "cottage industry" was never meant to describe. It has become myth. It has become a focus for nationalistic sentimentality, one of the things that "define us," as the chattering classes like to say.

The cottage has become real estate. It has become an environmental battleground. It has become other kinds of battleground as well, a battle between those who love peace and quiet and canoes, and those who love excitement and power tools and personal watercraft.

In 1989 there wasn't even a generic name for those things that buzzed around in the water. We called them Jet Skis or Sea-Doos or whatever. Then they multiplied, the way obnoxious machines do, until there were so many of them that it was necessary to invent a name for them, other than "those naughty things." Now they are personal watercraft, and calling them that, dull as it sounds, didn't seem to stop the spread of them. There are more than ever, although some say the new ones are quieter.

Many of the changes to the cottage simply reflect the changes in society. Cellphones are everywhere in the real world and they are everywhere in cottage country. That means people, particularly teenagers, are less isolated from each other. It also means that people who get lost on the way can call and say they are lost.

In 1989 there was no such thing as email, at least not as far as the vast majority of us were concerned. Now, if we choose to and have the right hookup, we can check it before smelling the outhouse. In fact, we can use the Internet to research the outhouse smell. We can do that for hours, in fact, to stall off doing anything about it.

There didn't use to be same-sex marriage. Well, there was, but it wasn't called that and society as a whole didn't think about it. Now same-sex couples are doing what opposite-sex couples do: they are looking for cottages. Perhaps they are buying all the requisite gear to engage in competitive bird-watching, something that has emerged in recent years too.

In society as a whole, people are getting older. Consequently, they want more comforts and fewer inconveniences. They want more of the labour-saving devices that are available in the city. And they want more golf courses. We are seeing that in cottage country. Soon we may see a boom in labour-saving golf courses.

At one and the same time, the cottage has become romanticized and it has become commercialized. The two feed on each other. The more love we focus on the cottage, either as a concept or a physical place, the more we want to spend on it. And the larger the idea of the cottage looms in our national sentiment, the more desirable it becomes as a piece of real estate, a setting for the latest in decor and gadgetry and barbecue recipes.

Hey, we live in a capitalist society. That's what happens. Which isn't to say that we can't wait to get there around the twenty-fourth of May.

Part 1

The Cottage: A Progress Report

Getting There Is
One-Quarter the Fun

So let's get going, shall we, down the old familiar road. Pack up the old jalopy and hit the highway. However, let's suppose, for the sake of argument, that we haven't been down that road for a few years. If we haven't, we might find things a bit different.

For a start, the old jalopy is a lot bigger, a van sort of thing, not much fun to drive, but it has to be that big because we are putting more things into it. There are golf clubs now, and wetsuits and CD players and laptop computers and various types of electronic gear. There are cases of bottled water, something we didn't think about years ago. Why would we?

There seems to be a greater variety of food and wine in the van, maybe because there is more storage space for it. And ingredients: you've never seen so many ingredients in one place. The thing about the van is you just throw in all this stuff, not bothering with things like suitcases. Remember suitcases? Without suitcases, you notice the clothes – a lot more of them, hiking gear and workout gear and fishing gear and jackets that breathe and shirts that dry fast and boots for this and that.

Fortunately, there's still room for the dog, but the dog has gear too.

Anyway, it's good to have the van packed and ready to go, particularly after the long argument about when to do it. There are lots of places where such a discussion doesn't happen – such as in a small town where the cottage is just down the road a bit – but around the big cities, getting to the cottage demands Strategy. We don't just pack the vehicle and go. No, we Plan.

Is three o'clock early enough to beat the traffic? No. And two isn't either? Can you get off work at eleven in the morning? Maybe that will beat the traffic? Can't do it? Well, maybe we should wait until tonight. Say nine o'clock. Then all the traffic will be over. But then again, maybe everybody's thinking that. So here's an idea. Why don't we leave right in the middle of rush hour. Nobody will be thinking of that. It's so crazy it might just work.

But it doesn't, of course. Rush hour is always rush hour. Except that these days a lot of hours that aren't supposed to be rush are.

What about phoning in sick and leaving on Thursday? Actually, what about going to the cottage on Tuesday and coming back on Friday, against the traffic, and staying in the city on the weekend?

You know someone is in fact doing that, because cottage commuters think of everything. They have tried everything and nothing works, except by total fluke: some days there's nothing on the road and you have clear sailing, and you have no idea why. The next week you leave at the same time and it's hell on wheels.

Off we go, whenever it is, the strategizing continuing, driving crosstown instead of uptown, because everybody else will be driving uptown instead of crosstown, except that we forgot about the construction at the bridge, as did several hundred other drivers, and there we are, stuck, with hours to go before we get there, with excited children in the van and an excited dog, and we're not even out of the city yet. We're not even within shouting distance of being out of the city yet.

With regard to shouting, perhaps one of us is making the

mistake of reminding another one of us about saying a few hours ago that we should have left earlier, or later, or yesterday, or tomorrow.

In our minds, though, we're still convinced it's worth it. Once we get on the highway and into the country, the old joy of driving to the cottage will return.

The highway, which we finally reach an hour or so later, is not the delightful country road we remember, with barns and cows, and clouds floating lazily in the blue sky. Now it's four lanes of apparently crazed idiots, going too slow and then going too fast, passing when they shouldn't, clenching their teeth, unless they are talking on the phone. It is hard to believe that all of these people share with us a simple yearning for a few days of peace and quiet under blue skies beside the water. When they get their old clothes on and a beer in their hand, they'll be just as calm as we would like to be right now.

We remember how it was fifteen years ago, when all we wanted was for that slow and crowded two-lane road to become four lanes so that we could get there faster. Now it's four lanes and it's just as slow and just as crowded and we can't wait until it ends and becomes two lanes again.

At least the kids aren't complaining about not being there yet. Now they're complaining because the movie they're watching on the back-seat DVD player is over and we haven't brought another one. We thought one would do it, and to tell the truth, we weren't happy even to bring that one. The kids, we explained quietly last night after they were in bed, should experience the scenery. They should experience the joy we once did of the trip to the cottage – watching for the first farms to appear, then the first big rocks, then that little lake on the left, the first of the lakes, then the halfway hamburger stop, then turning south onto the winding road, then the big tree after the red mailbox, then the dirt road, then . . . and then we'd be *there*!

Kids are different, it was explained to us. They want to watch movies. They know all about scenery. Scenery holds no mystery for them. They see it on the Internet. It's worth having a DVD player in the car to keep them happy, so they won't be all out of sorts when we get there.

On the highway, we watch the scenery and notice that where the first farms were are now shopping malls, a huge building at the side of the road with thirty-seven movie screens in it, beside which are four chain restaurants. The first big rocks are what used to be the second big rocks, the first having been removed to make way for two more lanes. The halfway hamburger joint is there, but closed and empty, and across the road from it is another chain restaurant, which the children urge us to stop at. We do, because we need to get gas anyway, the way this thing guzzles it, but we can't have that halfway hamburger because of the cholesterol. Instead of a halfway hamburger we have a halfway soy something.

At least we're halfway and the kids and the dog are holding up reasonably well. And eventually – not soon, but eventually – the traffic does thin out and the first little lake appears on the left. Wait a minute: wasn't the first little lake supposed to be *before* the halfway hamburger joint? Well, anyway, there it is, and nice to see it, although it seems to have houses all around it.

And here's the winding road. Kids, look – the winding road. THE WINDING ROAD! They seem to have straightened it out a little. The big tree must be along here somewhere. There's the red mailbox. That one over there, the blue one. And just around the corner should be . . . the . . . big . . . . . . stump.

Oh well. Here's the dirt road. Look, they've paved it. Any minute now we'll be there. Look, the Smiths have put up a No Trespassing sign. And was the Johnson place always called Chez Johnson?

Anyway, here we are. Everything else along the way was different, but here it's the same. The roof is sagging, there's a hornet's nest hanging from it, that tree looks like it might be dead, and watch out for the second step. Let's get the stuff in from the car. Nice to be here, isn't it? It was all worth it.

One Triumph after Another

Let's not forget why we loved the cottage in the first place. Let's not forget why we still go there, despite everything. Let's not forget what endures.

What endures is the outdoors, and being close to it. The pines still smell sweet, even on the most polluted of days. Some of us are closer to the outdoors than others. We sleep in tents or in drafty, unheated cabins with windows that never shut right. We know where on the floor to put the buckets when it rains. Others live in comfort, with double-glazed windows, heat when needed, and screened-in spaces for pre-dinner cocktails. But even for those people, the wild is still there. There is still weather. There is still fierce rain and thunderstorms and an actual fear that lightning could hit that big tree over there, which would then fall on the dock, crushing all the stuff that we should have picked up when it started raining.

The wild also includes the mice and the raccoons and even the bears and that large bird that everybody says is so rare but it won't shut up at six in the morning. Nature does not discriminate between rich cottager and poor cottager. The water is as cold for everybody.

But even that can be a blessing – that first leap in, and leap out, providing an opportunity for bragging rights, a chance, if you're small enough, or ancient enough, to be fussed over for a few precious minutes. It also provides an opportunity to enter into the lore, the discussion that comes up every year about how early or late it was when somebody jumped into the water, and who was that anyway?

The lore endures, in a way that it doesn't in town. How many accomplishments of this magnitude exist in the city? When was the last time anyone did anything legendary? You found a parking spot. You changed a fuse. More likely, you called a guy to come fix something, and it turned out all that was needed was to change a fuse. He looked at you like you were useless, which you were.

Whereas, at the cottage, your life is one triumph after another: jumping into cold water, retrieving a floating hat, diving to the bottom to save a sunken bar of soap, clearing a big branch off a path, chasing a bat out of the living room. And that's only the grown-ups. The children triumph several times before lunch. For them, life at the cottage is a parade of firsts. And each of these goes into the oral history of the place.

What endures is the way the kids react to being there. Their life may be an endless series of lessons and supervised activity at the club, or it may be aimless days of wandering in the woods and loafing at the beach. Either way, it's different from what they have the rest of the year and it makes them different people: more alive, more enthusiastic, more likely to communicate with their parents, more likely to sleep at night. In short, happy to be there.

It is their cottage memories, developed over just a few years, that create the culture and traditions of the place: the stops that must be made on the way there, the things that have to be done on first arrival, the meal that always has to be eaten on Friday night, the selection of the favourite tree, this year's demonstration of new accomplishments, such as jumping off the dock backwards.

In later years, as has always happened and probably always will, the kids as adults will try to pass these notions on to their children, who will be at first skeptical and then completely accepting and then dictatorial in forcing their parents to adhere to traditions that may be only a few months old.

How can you not love a place that has such an effect on children?

Scientists agree: The cottage is not the city

Not to mention you. No matter what has happened around you in seventeen years, no matter who has bought the place across the lake and put a wind turbine on it, your place still has the old effect on you. It slows down your heartbeat, stops you from walking and talking so fast, allows you to put your feet up and read a book. And that, to apply a sophisticated scientific analysis, is because the cottage is not the city.

It cuts a bit into the romanticizing that has grown up around the cottage in recent years, but one of the largest attractions of the cottage is not what it is, but what it isn't. The cottage isn't the city. It isn't a noisy, smelly place covered in pavement.

The cottage isn't that constant background noise you notice only on the first night when you return home. Even at two in the morning you hear it, the noise of constant traffic in the near distance, a noise you realize now has been completely absent from your life in the past few weeks.

The cottage isn't your cubicle, with the telephone always ringing and the email notification making that annoying little pinging noise. It isn't your backyard, with the neighbour's leaf blower in full operation. It isn't the traffic on the way home from work, where slow learners grapple with the apparently unsolvable problem of how to merge three lanes into two without everybody coming to a complete stop.

The cottage isn't a television set blaring. It isn't music nobody listens to in malls and restaurants and airports. It isn't your kids playing video games instead of making conversation.

It isn't no seat on the bus, no clerks in the store, no parking on the street between seven at night and seven in the morning, no parking on the street between seven in the morning and seven at night, no relief from the cheery voice that asks if this is Mr. or Mrs. Gordon and how are you today.

You would go anywhere to avoid all of that, and if you're lucky, you can. And if that anywhere has outdoor plumbing and mosquitoes and it gets cold at night and the nearest store is too far away and they don't have the newspaper anyway and it's hard to find a deck that has all fifty-two cards in it, plus jokers, and you might have read that book already last summer – well, at least it's not the city. All by itself, that's good.

The cottage can be full of anxiety for some people. They want it to be perfect, or at least as perfect as the one they were at last weekend, where the big party was. They worry about the zoning of that property across the lake. They don't like that sound the boat makes. They are alarmed about the mosquitoes, about acid rain, tent caterpillars, zebra mussels, and property taxes. They want their kids to have learning opportunities instead of lying around reading Harry Potter.

People like that shouldn't have cottages if they can't leave their anxiety behind. They should remain forever in the city, stay late at the office and check their BlackBerrys for messages in the odd moments filed under "Leisure" in their daily calendars. They wouldn't know what to do with a cottage, although they sorely need one. In August they could taste real blackberries.

For the rest of us, those cottage woes are manageable and, in the best cases, ignorable. They go with the territory. We learn to fix what really needs to be fixed, buy what really needs to be bought. We learn to adapt to a different pace and adapt to how the kids have adapted to a different pace, even if that means lying around inside on a perfectly nice day. We find it easy not to keep up with the Joneses. The Joneses aren't next door, after all; they're miles across the lake, and so what if their boat is bigger. It uses more gas and you can't see it from here anyway.

We learn, in fact, that our way is the best way, the way things have always been done, the way our grandparents did it, if we are lucky enough to have had grandparents who owned the place. So why would we want to have what the Joneses have? They don't have what we have. They don't have the crooked tree and the marshmallows on Wednesday nights and the around-the-island race in the dark.

It takes only a single summer to indoctrinate a new generation in these cottage ways, only a single summer to create an awareness that no summer property is complete without a crooked tree and all summers must have an around-the-island race in the dark. In a way that the city cannot manage, the cottage creates family tradition and family history. The traditions and the history endure, despite everything, despite the onrush of what passes for civilization and the dubious progress it brings.

That's why we loved the cottage in the first place. That's why we still do.

Here Comes the City

That having been said, there is no escaping the fact that the city is getting closer all the time. Even when it is several hundred kilometres away, it approaches, encroaches, makes its presence felt. Although many cottagers resent it, the fact is that we have brought the city with us, sometimes unwittingly, the way a boat from afar brings zebra mussels into a hitherto unspoiled lake.

At other times, the act of bringing the city is quite witting. We want what the city offers, we want it at the cottage, and we haven't yet realized that having the city at the cottage means we don't quite have the cottage anymore.

It is useful to think of cottage country as a kind of Third World tourist attraction – Bali, say. Unspoiled, it attracted thousands, then millions, drawn to its unspoiledness. They wanted to see beautiful sunsets and starlit night skies. They wanted to breathe clean air. They wanted to meet people who still retained the openness of an uncorrupted life.

So they came and they brought their cameras and their dollars and their enthusiasm for the way things were still done. But soon it became clear that taking pictures and meeting the inhabitants would not be enough. There had to be nice places to stay and there had to be good food to eat and, if it wasn't too much trouble, that food had to be a lot like food at home. There had to be air conditioning if possible, and there had to be something to do at night. A casino would be nice, or maybe a Vegas-style floor show at the hotel.

Meanwhile, all-news networks had frightened people so much about the inhabitants that the tourists no longer wanted to meet them at all, except maybe for having a few of them come to the hotel lobby and do a native dance.

There had to be some activity for the kids, since it wouldn't do to have them interacting with the inhabitants and they were too young for Vegas-style floor shows. A wax museum would be the bare minimum.

That's why you see many of the world's most beautiful places surrounded by American-style hotels, air-conditioned within an inch of their lives, the kids lounging by the pool playing video games or watching DVDs in the room, before going out to eat at McDonald's and then on to see wax sculptures of Hollywood movie stars and British politicians.

Is there a wax museum near your cottage yet? If not, it's only because the financing has not yet become available. Everything else is there, all brought to you by people who wanted to leave the city but couldn't bear to leave the city behind. The dire consequences of electricity – radio, television, electric can openers – have been well documented. But electricity has since been put to new and even more sinister uses. It is not just television now, but satellite television, advertised in one recent publication as follows: "Getting away from it all no longer means losing touch with what's happening and your world. Take the TV you love with you."

That was impossible a few years ago. If you had any TV at all at the cottage, it was not the TV you loved, if in fact you loved it in the first place. It ran off rabbit ears, or perhaps one of those huge ugly towers, and it pulled in hazy, blurred, and distorted images of the TV you used to love when you were back in the city and had cable. This could be avoided by putting one of those huge ugly satellite dishes on your shoreline, indelibly branding yourself as a nouveau riche city slicker to those who passed by.

But progress never sleeps, and apparently the new dishes are so small you could hide them among the . . . um, dishes. This means taking the TV you love with you and it means, more significantly, taking the TV your kids love with you, which means that their friends who don't have the TV they love at their places will be over, watching at your place, especially on sunny days, for some reason.

Wanting to get the kids out of the cottage is the kind of thing that could, in fact, make parents wish for a wax museum. And were there a wax museum, they could drive the kids to it, because the roads have really improved. It wouldn't be cottage country without good roads, we now think, because there's the casino to go to and the golf course, either the close one or the not-so-close one.

It does not seem unreasonable to people anymore that they should now have a nicely paved driveway at the cottage, since the car is there anyway. And a garage? – might as well.

The people on the islands can't have nice driveways, but they can do other things, such as build grand docks and large decks and put up bright lights. And they can afford it.

The big difference between cottage country now and cottage country a couple of decades ago is money. People with cottages have more money to spend on them now, or at least are willing to spend more money, even if they don't have it. The result is the same and the result is not good. Early cottagers, the ones we grew up emulating, thought of the cottage as a place where money was unimportant, a democratic place where people all dressed the same and it didn't matter how important or unimportant you were in your city life. What mattered was whether you were, in the cottage vernacular, a good camper – could you fish, chop, cook on a wood stove, find a path, endure a bee sting, drag a branch off the roof?

Mind you, there were always big cottages and little cottages, but the money didn't show itself then like it does now.

The thin edge of the lawn

People from the city miss a nice lawn. After all, they have one in town, why shouldn't they have one out here, where there's all this scenery and the trees and all the things that make a lawn look nicer? A good lawn takes a certain amount of maintenance, and there's the lawnmower to buy, a good, big one, since there's so much lawn. Then there's the shed to put up to hold the lawnmower and the gasoline. It all starts with the lawn, which will receive further care in the next chapter.

The impulse behind it all is pleasant, yet insidious: things that are nice in the city would be even nicer at the cottage, so why not import them? If it is nice to read the newspaper over your morning coffee in the city, how much nicer to do so at the cottage. Thus, a prosperous little enterprise begins, delivering newspapers to the dock, with the result that people who should really, for their mental health, be taking a time out from the news are reading it first thing and getting steamed.

And if a cultural evening is enjoyable in the city, how much more enjoyable it would be among the trees and the breeze beside the lake. So cottage country adds culture too, importing literary festivals and highbrow musical events.

The young people need entertaining too, as do the tourists, so rock concerts and fairs are added, the fairs no longer concerned with selling local produce and very much concerned with loud music and fast rides.

It all adds up. Soon there is nothing you could get in the city that you can't get in cottage country. The city has arrived, or is so close to actually arriving that cottage country now resembles a suburb. It has family restaurants and shopping centres. It has houses and lawns and garages. It also has true cottagers, who keep coming back, keep hoping that the city will go away and let the cottage be the cottage again.

They think of themselves as true cottagers anyway. Of course, has anyone ever thought of himself as a false cottager?

Nature Is Nice, but It Could Use a Little Touch-Up

In the early years of our nationhood, Canadians concentrated on conquering our environment. We chopped down trees to make farms, blasted through rock to make roads and railways. We fashioned great cities and not-so-great cities. We built shelter from the cold.

Conquering the environment is no laughing matter, and we learned to rest from it. We invented the cottage, and it was quite a clever idea: after spending most of our days trying to conquer the environment, we would spend at least a few each year letting the environment conquer us.

Instead of building bridges over the water, we would swim in it. Instead of cutting down trees, we would lie under them and look up. Instead of hunting wild animals, we would show them off to our children, if they were small enough and didn't bite – the animals, that is.

Instead of taming the wild, we would make ourselves wilder. We would live with the heat and cold, whichever it happened to be. Shaving would pause, sloppy clothes would emerge, dirt would be accepted, sweat would be just fine. It would all be a nice contrast to what we did the rest of the year, and when we went back to our rest-of-the-year lives, as we would have to do, we would feel refreshed and somehow fortified.

Our physical surroundings reflected this thought. A cottage, no matter how large, was a minimal structure, intended primarily to keep out the rain and the mosquitoes and provide a place to store bathing suits and mismatched badminton racquets. It had just enough of a stove, just enough of a bathroom, though that might be located a ways off in the woods. It had just enough of a boat with just enough of a dock with probably no dock furniture on it.

The area surrounding the cottage was about the way we found it, or our great-grandfathers found it. There were primitive little paths to get us to dock or outhouse. At some stage a tree or two might have had to be cut to make the paths. Each year a few bushes would be trimmed to keep it open. If a tree fell, it would be dragged out of the way and cut up for firewood. If a tree didn't fall, it would be left alone. Sometimes a path would be rerouted to get around a tree.

As a reward for our benign neglect, nature rewarded us amply, with beautiful trees and wildflowers, birds overhead, the sound of water lapping against the rocks on the shore, ferns and weeds and toadstools, the whistle of the wind, the glories of thunderstorms. It would be difficult to improve on this. But some of us feel the need to try.

It's hard to say if it's the majority; many of us still prefer to take the outdoors as we find it. We think it might be nice to have a little patch of grass to play badminton on; we worry about the gradual erosion of the shoreline; we look for a spot of colour other than green. Mostly, we're content.

But the urge to improve is primal in some of us. You have only to count the dumpsters in your neighbourhood at home, watch that lovely old front porch come off, see that little scruffy patch of weeds replaced with red chips of bark and perfectly formed boulders purchased from Mr. Boulder, the tree in the front yard coming down to make way for a semicircular driveway – you have only to look around you to see that we are not, as a people, always content with what we find.

Fair enough, you might say. And it's not that there isn't some work to be done. That old cottage is severely leaning. Mosquitoes fly in through the cracks in the boards, mice also find their way in, pots and pans have to be strategically placed on the living-room floor to catch the rain, and the outhouse smells worse than an outhouse.

It has to be fixed, no question, maybe even rebuilt from the ground up. But does that new structure, when it is finished, need a *lawn*? There was never a lawn before. There are no lawns in nature. Grass, yes, but not lawns. Lawns need mowing, which means more smelly gasoline, more noise. Lawns need chemicals. Or at least people think lawns need chemicals. Lawns need various unpleasant gadgets to discourage moles and groundhogs.

Lawns need work.

But people need lawns. Why? Because lawns represent beauty to them. They are at a beautiful place, the cottage, and they just want to make it a bit more beautiful. So put a lawn in. Just get rid of a few trees and bushes and some large rocks. There.

Now, what else? Well, you know the way the water splashes onto the rocks and makes that annoying gurgling noise at night and some of the shoreline gets pulled away each year and rocks and debris wash up? You could put a wall there to prevent that. Thousands have. Just a little low wall to keep the water away from the shoreline.

It's simply a matter of applying the reno mentality that works so well in the city.

Decking, for example. You know how bumpy the walk down to the dock is, and how Cindy twisted her ankle three summers ago, or was it four? You could deck over that, make a nice boardwalk. It could run from the dock to the main deck. And, come to think of it, you could expand that deck a bit, to bring it closer to the dock. So that the deck becomes an extension of the dock and the dock the deck. All that would have to come out would be a few bushes and some more rocks. The new cedar decking looks so nice against the trees, and it will be such a comfort to the old people not to have to walk on the ground, where there might be a root.

There's no reason, when you think about it, to confine the decking to the house. There's that nice point, the one that juts out a bit where you like to go to look at the sunset. You could put a deck there too. Then you could put some nice furniture on it. It's not as if when you cover over one rock there won't be another one.

What next? What about painting the place? The colour it is now, the dark brown, it was fine for the older generation; they said they didn't want the place to stick out too much. But hey, what's the point of spending all this dough on renovations if nobody is going to see them? Something in a blue would show up well, and there are shades of salmon that are quite acceptable among designers now.

You see where it leads. The unfortunate fact is that it is human nature to have a slightly adversarial relationship with non-human nature. The day after the lily was invented somebody showed up wanting to gild it. Today a plain old gilded lily is nothing. There are gilded lily candelabras, gilded lily radios, gilded lily bathroom fixtures, hand-painted gilded lilies. Gilded lilies are better than ever.

You can look up from where you sit right now and see nothing but trees and water. The water is blue – nothing you can do about that – and the trees are green. Nothing but blue and green. But when you look more closely, there are shades of green. Lots and lots of shades of green. The shadows create shades; the different types of trees are their own shades. The bushes are all different shades. It's actually quite a nice view from where you are.

But someone wants to make it better by hanging a plant right in your line of sight.

That would be a pretty pink thing, a petunia or something, in a pot purchased from a wonderful craftsperson in the market. He sold several similar ones, all quite nice, and there's one right outside the kitchen window so you can see it while you're doing the dishes, one on the steps, with the three smaller ones, the other just around the corner by the barbecue. If you can get over the idea that someone is trying to decorate the outdoors, they look all right.

Just as the flower garden looks all right. Flower gardens always look all right. They look especially all right in areas, such as cities, that desperately need flowers. They even look all right beside lawns, which get a bit monotonous too, if the truth be told.

Putting in the lawn sort of made the flower garden inevitable, didn't it? And that made the sprinkler system necessary, which caused the upgrade in the pump. Improving nature comes at a price.

Studying things at the cottage: A case study

As if to justify this vast investment in nature, a certain seriousness of purpose has descended on the new cottager's contemplation of it. The cottager once looked at the moon, noted that it was bright, or half or red or hazy or full, then summoned a co-cottager to share the view, perhaps with some form of ulterior motive. "Look at the moon," he would say. "Isn't it lovely?" she would reply and that would be that, except for the ulterior stuff.

The modern cottager *studies* the moon. He has a telescope. He has a moon book. This is the best possible place for viewing the moon, and the opportunity shouldn't be wasted. There is a lot to be learned about the moon.

Organized moon walks are available, enabling groups to walk, in safety, to designated moon-viewing areas, where trained guides can inform them of various aspects of interest. There is much more to the moon than it looking pretty, if you only take the time to learn.

The modern cottager studies the animals too, through such vehicles as the nighttime wolf howl, in which guides take unsuspecting cottagers into the night, then lead them in howls that might elicit a wolfly response. Sometimes there is one and sometimes it's just the guys drinking beer down the lake who kind of sound that way. Sometimes it's a guide from a competing wolf tour. It's pretty thrilling anyway, although nowhere near as thrilling as not being part of a tour and hearing a noise in the bushes that might be a wolf. There is something to be said for the pleasures of innocence.

The precedent for such activities was established several years ago by those who learned that people would pay to sit on buses and look at trees turn red. This activity was given a more dignified name – the Fall Colours Tour – and now each year thousands of people fork over hard-earned dollars, dollars that would buy many hanging plants, in order to journey to places not too far away where the leaves on the trees are pretty much the same colour as the leaves closer to home but maybe a bit brighter, and you get to stay in a nice hotel before getting on the bus to go out to see them.

Once the serious consequences of leaves falling were recognized, it was not long before other aspects of nature, formerly taken for granted, were submitted to scholarly gazes. Nature walks were organized, enabling cottagers to leave their own part of nature to walk in another part of nature that looked exactly the same but was a few miles down the road.

There were economic consequences as well. Birding, formerly birdwatching, became big business. Telescopes turned up at the Canadian Tire. Fishing went on television. Gardening got its own section in the bookstore. It also got its own hats, gloves, exercises for the back, and devices that helped you avoid bending over.

It turns out that there was not a single piece of cottage country nature that did not have educational value. And where educational value could be established, tours could be organized, gear manufactured, how-to books written, published, and sold.

The primitive cottager just went to the cottage without learning about it. He swam without knowing the exact temperature of the water. He walked in the woods without having read the book. He swam at the beach, but what did he really know about sand anyway? The new cottager takes the moon seriously and on nights when it shines in a merely ordinary way, he decorates it by shooting fireworks into the sky, after carefully reading the instructions.

Cottage Sports

Part 1: Can the Cottage Survive Golf?

Few would think, on a sunny day, strolling across the lush acres of grass, enjoying the warm afterglow of a six-iron that landed on the green and miraculously stayed there – few would think that they are willing accomplices in the creation of one of the most serious menaces to the survival of cottage civilization as we have known it.

The golf course is the enemy of the cottage, yet golfers don't realize it. Blithely holing out from fifteen feet or bitterly thrashing through the underbrush in search of a duck-hooked Pinnacle 4, they are part of the problem, even though they think they are part of the solution.

"Nice to get away for a few hours, get out of peoples' hair, rest up so we can tackle the boathouse door tomorrow," they think, as they shine up their clubs. Meanwhile, the cottage culture they love so much continues to fight a losing battle against the slow but steady invasion of a large grassy mass, its vast green surface broken only by occasional infusions of sand and plastic toilet structures. It is desertification in reverse, a takeover by grass.

How could golfers not know this is so? How could they,

smiling in their comfortable slacks, the colours of fruit, not know the threat they pose?

The answer is only too obvious. They cannot know because they are obsessed with something else. Obsessed with the fact that the ball too frequently skitters along the ground and over the green, when it is supposed to float gently into the air and come to rest lightly, stopping inches from the hole, as it does on TV – obsessed in this way, they are unable to consider any but the most immediate consequences.

Let us list those long-run consequences anyway, just in case a golfer somewhere has the energy to read something after a hard day at the links and is too lazy to get out of his chair to find the golf magazine across the room.

1. Loss of acreage. This is the most obvious one. New golf courses are being built every year in the scenic areas where cottagers gather. Golf courses take up a lot of room that could be used by ducks, foxes, wildflowers, and little kids exploring in the woods. The demand for cottage property is exploding, and golf courses are taking potential cottage property away.

2. Loss of productivity. The cottage does not run on its own. There are chores to be done: docks to be fixed, things to be taken to the dump, odd scratching sounds to investigate, that overhanging branch, screens to be mended, and that roaring in the boat engine that you'd always promised to do something about. And you're going to take off for five hours – six, if you count getting to the course and back. And when you return, are you going to be invigorated and ready to get at the chores that need to be done? No, you're going to have a nap because you're tired and your back hurts.

3. Environmental damage. Every single golf course in sight these days claims not to use harmful chemicals to keep the grass in the lush state that golfers expect, having looked at golf courses on TV. Taking the proprietors at their word, and not worrying about past practices either, it is still necessary to point out that the land was not meant to be this way, with grass

instead of grasses, trees eliminated, bushes hacked away, huge parking lots carved out of the forest, artificial ponds created with clever little bridges over them, made out of stone blasted from the hills, little white vehicles buzzing back and forth across the fairways, animals driven off, except for Canada geese, who seem to have been attracted from afar.

Actually, this last is an environmental plus, since Canada geese are widely regarded as much more attractive in flight than not. Having them centrally located on a golf course instead of scattered about on hundreds of docks and decks is of considerable benefit to the cottage way of life.

But let's not forget, either, the thousands of litres of water sucked out of the lakes and rivers in order to keep those fairways and greens lush and soft. Some day we might wish we had it back.

4. Threat to family life. Cottagers have obligations to others in their family: their children, their parents, their aunts, uncles, and cousins. Children, especially, need adult attention, not just to keep them from rolling in the poison ivy, but also to notice their accomplishments, to praise their ability to jump backwards off the dock, or to offer information about the crawly thing they just found in the bushes. Children need to be read to. Cooks need to be kept company in the kitchen. Grandparents need to be listened to.

Man, woman, or child, the golfer is incapable of doing any of these. For one thing, the golfer is not there. For another, when the golfer returns, he or she is likely to be incapable of rational conversation, too tired to pay attention to the needs of others, or unable to discuss anything other than the five-wood that just cleared the trap and might have gone right into the hole if they hadn't put it at the back of the green this time.

5. Threat to morale. The moods of golfers are well known. They begin with an inattentiveness in the hours preceding the game, as the golfer cleans spikes, counts balls, polishes irons, and makes swinglike motions while others are planning family expeditions to the beach. The mood swings continue at the

course, where they can't do anybody any harm, aside from those in the immediate vicinity.

There is a fruitful area of social-science research here, testing the hypothesis of a correlation between mood swings and golf swings. If the latter did not exist, would the former?

When the golfer returns to the cottage, likely depressed and certainly tired, more damage is done. The golfer spreads gloom, unless he or she has the good sense to withdraw to a quiet place and study the diagrams in golf magazines instead of attempting conversation with other humans. Thus, the golfer's kin are spared his or her moodiness, but they are also deprived of the golfer's presence, which, in happier days, can even be pleasant.

At the more fortunate cottages, one day can be the beginning and end of it, as the golfer quickly recovers from this, his only game of the year, and makes a re-entry into normal life. But that doesn't always happen. In far too many cases, the golfer, thinking of himself as on vacation and having lots of free time, soon has more games scheduled. In such cases, the gloom is succeeded the next day by a lifting of mood that, it turns out, has to do with the golfer's discovery, while thinking about it in the middle of the night, of an adjustment to his swing that should fix everything and that he is anxious to try, perhaps later today, since the boathouse door can wait.

None of this would have happened had that 150 acres of scrubland down at the end of the lake not been turned into a golf course. When you think about it, 150 acres of scrubland never hurt anybody.

Invoking the boathouse door rule

A less publicized threat posed by cottage golf is the threat to golf itself. Those who love the game for the purity of its rules and the solemn adherence to its traditions can only be horrified at the modifications that are made in the cottage country game.

Some changes, to be sure, can be seen as positive, in that they represent a victory for populist democracy over aristocratic stodginess. The bending of the golf dress code falls into this category. Whereas the city golfer at an established club must wear a shirt with a collar, socks that are just so, shorts that are not too short and don't have any pockets on the outside, whereas the city golfer must avoid logos that are not strictly associated with golf, the cottage golfer wears just about anything. That old Montreal Expos cap, the traditional tricolour one, is just fine; any shirt with sleeves is okay, including that one from the last Eagles reunion tour; any shoes will work, except for the 1985 golf shoes with the metal spikes; and the length of shorts is up to the conscience of the wearer. All of this is to the good, in that it makes golfers resemble normal human beings.

It may also be seen as a positive development that conceded putts on a cottage golf course are considerably longer than those in other jurisdictions. Among serious city golfers, a ball has to be within, say, eighteen inches of the hole for the putt to be conceded. On the cottage course, putts of three or even four feet are considered gimmes. Sometimes this is justified because of impending darkness, or simply the need to speed up the game in order to get back for the boathouse door repairs. But the main, unspoken reason is to eliminate at least one of the causes of the cottage golfer's dark mood. There is nothing like a missed four-foot putt to ruin a golfer's day, and when his day (or her day) is ruined, so are the days of those near and dear. Often the nights are ruined too. To avert that, the four-footer is conceded, so that it will not be missed. This leaves it to the cottage golfer to find other ways to ruin his day. Unfortunately, golf provides many others.

If purists consider the conceded four-footer an affront to the game, this is not the only one. The lie of the ball on the fairway, and even in the rough, is routinely improved, on the grounds that the course is not in good shape this year, owing to the absence of rain or the presence of too much of it. Other affronts are made necessary by the nature of cottage course terrain. In the Canadian Shield, the rough is not a place of slightly longer grass and a few stately oaks. In the Canadian Shield, the rough has dense bush, more pines and spruce than you can count. Where there are no trees, there is rock, which makes a distinctive sound when a ball strikes it. It is not at all the same sound as is made by the ball striking a pine tree, or two.

Looking for the ball, a time-honoured – well, not exactly honoured – feature of golf, takes on a different dimension in the cottage game. It is done more quickly and with considerably less optimism. In addition to the rocks, there are mosquitoes and black flies, in season; there is the possibility, in certain areas, of bears and even cougars. There is poison ivy, the rare snake, and lots of stuff that isn't harmful, but really scratches.

Modifications to the rules arise out of this. One is that a ball found in the area where your ball disappeared is deemed to be yours. Some have qualms accepting this when the ball that disappeared is white and the ball that is discovered is orange, but moral misgivings are easily swallowed when the alternative is a two-stroke penalty for a lost ball.

Even that two-stroke penalty is by no means a sure thing. Often it is replaced by a one-stroke penalty, on the grounds that professional golfers have people to help them find balls and if you and I had those people helping us, we'd find the ball, so let's assume we found it and charge one stroke for tossing it onto the fairway.

Further, in games where impending darkness is a factor, balls are never lost. They are simply replaced without penalty, the logic being that the original ball would have been found in proper light and it is important to get the round over with to avoid having to drive the boat back in the dark, so why don't you just play another one and don't count it.

Certain local wrinkles can be applied with enthusiasm. In Kenora, Ontario, the scorecard states that a ball stolen by a fox can be replaced without penalty and some courses in the Rockies have sympathetic rules relating to bear avoidance. Ravens are another hazard, Canada geese have been mentioned, and there are probably critters thought to be at work in other jurisdictions, all of them combining to reduce the scores of the aggrieved golfers.

In not too many years, cottage golf in North America may adopt some of the innovative practices of golf in Australia, where genuine peril does lurk in the rough, mostly in the form of snakes, but also spiders and the occasional crocodile, and no lost ball is ever looked for. Instead of the two-stroke penalty for a lost ball, a one-stroke penalty applies. When that Australian notion comes to North America, our cottage golfer's creativity may invent a rationalization for eliminating even that small penalty.

In such ways does golf become not only an affront to the cottage, but an affront to itself. But, like the cottage, golf will continue, a symbol of some irrational, but compelling force. A noted cottage golfer, Stephen Leacock, once suggested that golf is not a game at all, but "a form of moral effort." You can imagine what his boathouse door looked like.

Part 2: Can Tennis Survive the Cottage?

Unlike golf, in which the participant plays mostly against his inner demons and thus can hurt only his own feelings, tennis requires a real opponent. Therefore, there will be attempts to hit the ball past the real opponent, perhaps even *at* the real opponent, if the real opponent is a bit too aggressive at the net. The real opponent's wimpy little second serve will be taken advantage of. The real opponent's bad knee will be tested by making the real opponent run a bit.

It goes without saying that bad feelings can result from this. When competitive juices flow, it happens. In the real world, the consequences are neither severe nor long-lasting. But in cottage tennis, the real opponent may well be a relative, who cannot be avoided, especially in the short run.

That is why cottage tennis requires particular skills and sensibilities. Winning the game is not always the most important thing. In fact, it may be the worst thing that could happen.

If, for example, the opponent belongs to that rare breed that owns its own tennis court, certain rules apply. First off, resist the urge to take off your cap and tug your forelock when your opponent appears. The court is probably one hundred years old, and he had nothing to do with having it built. If, in fact, he did have it built, then he's the one responsible for all that construction racket you heard last summer. So you have the moral high ground there.

This does not, however, give you the right to whup your opponent. There is nothing quite so demoralizing as to be whupped on one's personal facility, so you should keep that in mind if you want the friendship to continue. If you don't care about the friendship, then by all means use the drop shot, especially if he's overweight.

Assuming that you value the friendship, remember that he takes pride in his court and in his knowledge of its little bumps and cracks and how to play them. Losing under such circumstances does little permanent damage to your reputation or your self-image.

In most cases, however, you will be playing on public courts at some recreational facility. Chances are that the courts will not be in good repair, because tennis in recent years has been assigned a low priority by those who do the assigning. That means little bits of grass will be poking through the service line and there will be a crack right about where your opponent's serve lands in the add court. Funny bounces will occur, and these are to be taken with good grace.

Since the cottage is thought of as a break from reality and cottage tennis is thought of as a break from the small amount of reality that exists at the cottage, it is very unwise to bring your temper to it. A loud curse at a bad bounce will constitute an incident, and will likely be discussed at dinner, where you will all be. Even if the bad bounce costs you the second set, you have to pretend to be amused by it. Either that or have the summer of 2006 go down in cottage lore as "The year Charley lost it on the tennis court."

It is also possible to distinguish yourself in a negative way by how you dress. Great care has to be taken here. Despite the informality of cottage country, some courts keep the old tradition of requiring that white be worn. In most cases, that tradition has been stretched a bit, and now you can wear just about any kind of shirt, if it has a collar and something resembling sleeves and doesn't have the logo of a motorcycle gang on the chest or sayings relating to sexual prowess. Just so long as your shoes are white.

It is also good to have real tennis shoes, since the kind you usually bum around in might dig up the court. True, most cottage country courts are concrete painted green and not easily dug up, but it's better to be on the safe side. Nothing is more humiliating than being thrown off a tennis court for having the wrong shoes or wearing the slogan of a swingers' club on your T-shirt. The year that happened to you would go down in cottage lore too.

On the other hand, if you show up all dressed in white, your shirt sporting the logo of a posh midtown club, you will be considered to be a bit of a fancy Dan, and your game had better be awfully good.

If you do in fact belong to a posh midtown club, it is likely that you have a tennis bag emblazoned with the posh midtown tennis club logo. Since it is the only tennis bag you own, you are within your rights to carry it. But carrying your usual two racquets inside it is unacceptable.

It is a good idea to remember that all games will be closely watched, not only by those involved in them, but by those who are waiting for the court, who will also know you or know enough about you to be able to speak critically about your game at the earliest opportunity.

Games will be conducted in an atmosphere of mock competitiveness. This allows for people to actually try and even to celebrate their good shots, as long as they don't appear that serious about it. Similarly, manoeuvres aimed at actually winning a point are allowed, if conducted with an air of detachment. Winning is fine; visibly wanting to win is not.

The perils of mixed doubles

None of this is easy, and there are many reasons to opt for a nap instead. One is to avoid getting involved in a mixed doubles

game. In a mixed doubles game, your spouse is either going to
be your partner or your opponent. Neither is better than the
other. If your spouse is your partner, you are going to embar-
rass him or her either by losing or by winning inappropriately.
If your spouse is your opponent, you are going to alienate him
or her either by defeating him or her or by hitting him or her
with the ball. (This last is also possible when your spouse is
your partner, when you serve right into his or her back while
he or she stands at the net. Don't let the year 2006 go into the
cottage annals as the year you did that.)

Most games of mixed doubles arise from an innocent suggestion – to wit: "Why don't we all play tennis?" This seems
like a good idea to everyone at the time, since people are not
thinking of the possible pitfalls, only of hitting the ball and
getting some exercise. Inevitably, however, wide disparities in
the levels of play will emerge, often in the warm-up. The usual
way to resolve these is to pair the worst player with the best
player. However, it is never wise to state it that way, particularly if people don't know one another all that well. And also if
they do.

Several challenges arise. The opponents of the team with
the worst player will want to hit the ball to him all the time, so
as to win the match. But that would appear to be bad sports-
manship. So they have to make sure to hit it to him only at the
most crucial moments and make at least some of those strokes
appear as mistakes.

The partner of the worst player has challenges of her own.
She has to applaud and encourage him. Saying "Nice try!" is
always good, although it gets to be a bit wearing after the first
one hundred or so times. She also has to avoid seeming to hog
all the shots, while, at the same time, hogging all the shots, so
as not to lose. Since the opponents are hitting to him all the
time, this is doubly difficult.

The easiest position to be in, ironically, is that of the worst
player. No one expects anything from you. Every half-decent,

or at least not wretched, shot you hit is enthusiastically applauded. You don't have to run for too many balls, since your partner will be happy to do that. The only thing to remember is not to apologize and to wear something white.

Part 3: Can Fishing Survive the Fisherman?

There will also be fishermen and -women (only the CBC calls them "fishers"). And there will always, one can hope, be fish. But the fishing environment has changed in many ways, the biggest one being the disappearance of the casual fisherman.

You were probably one yourself – took a few casts off the dock when there was nothing much else to do, or went out in the boat on a calm evening, or even the afternoon, mostly for the nice feeling of being out in the boat. But you'd take along a rod and a companion. One of you would drive, or row, or paddle, and the other would fish, trolling along the shoreline for an hour or two, not really expecting to catch much and delighted if you caught anything.

A terrific fuss would ensue if you arrived back with a fish. Photographs would be taken, maybe even old, rusty scales produced if the fish looked like it might be larger than usual. Someone would know how to fillet the fish and it would form part of a meal the next day.

If you didn't catch a fish, you would at least have had a nice time on the lake, checking out the sunset, watching a heron, seeing the beaver do his classic swim across the horizon at dusk.

There was always somebody more fanatical than that about fishing. Fishing could be studied, the practice of it made more systematic. Instead of doing what you always did, the serious fisherman would try different lures, different depths. He or she knew the likely places and how to cast into them. The reel would be kept well oiled. The trips out on the lake would be made before breakfast, when the fish were most likely to be hungry too.

There was an element of art in this kind of fishing, a combination of knowledge, skill, and instinct. It was carried out at a slow and methodical pace. Fishing at a high level took patience.

Now it takes technology. Machines take the depth of the water for the new fisherman. Machines find the fish. The well-equipped boat has such machines. The well-equipped boat also goes like stink, speeding across the lake from one likely spot to another, without pausing to take heed of the sunset or the heron. Fishing is more scientific than it used to be, but less deliberate. It is about catching fish, and perhaps only about that.

As we know, an industry has developed around this kind of fishing, and any cottage community of any size has an annual fishing derby with valuable prizes put up by corporate sponsors. The local economy benefits from the influx of fishermen, and who can argue with that? Not even the fish would argue much (and you know how argumentative fish usually are!), since those unlucky enough to be caught are snagged on barbless hooks and released alive.

While fishing at this high level has boomed, fishing at the casual level seems to have declined. It's hard to know why this is so. The competitive fishermen are not getting in the way of the casual ones. There is no war between them.

Nor are the competitive fishermen to blame if there seem to be fewer fish in the lake. They put the fish back, after all. If there are fewer fish, there are more serious villains, corporate and governmental, than competitive fishermen.

So where have the casual fishermen gone? Or why have they gone?

Maybe it's just that fishing has suddenly become too serious. You need a licence to do it now, in most places. The licence is not expensive; it's only a nuisance, but it serves as a reminder that fishing is not some casual endeavour.

More important, maybe the romance has gone out of it. The knowledge that someone can locate fish with an instrument in his boat takes away that sense that instinct and, yes, luck are involved.

It used to be that when two fishing boats met on the lake, the customary greeting was "Any luck?" Now we know that luck has nothing to do with it. Rather than spending time on the lake greeting fellow fishermen with "Any science?" we decide to do something else.

A Cottage for Sale

Through the generations the cottage has united families. Much of the gooey writing we see about cottages in magazines is a celebration of family. They never see each other during the year, and then, for a blissful two weeks or so in the summer, they are together, working together, living in harmony, laughing over the old cottage memories, shedding a tear under a pine tree for a departed relative.

It's all true too, which is why we see so much of it. If cottages were not good for families, no one would go to them except hermits wanting to escape their families. There are some of those, but they are in the minority. The rest of us happily unite each summer with our sisters and brothers, cousins and uncles and aunts. The grandparents and grandchildren enjoy one another's company. It's like Christmas, but better because there is not the tension involved in elaborate meal planning and gift giving, there is less drinking, and there is no need, most days, for overcoats.

Despite the changes that have come to cottage country, the desire to keep the cottage going, to keep it in the family, continues. We see that in all the complicated and scary articles about estate planning and dealing with capital gains tax and establishing legal structures that will enable the cottage to survive. People are thinking about it all the time, and not always with smiles on their faces.

Some are smiling, though, at the thought of money to be made. Cottages are hot, everybody wants one, and since cottages close to large cities are scarce, the prices are skyrocketing. Suddenly, the cottage is an extremely valuable commodity. Ironically, one of the biggest threats to the cottage's survival is the popularity of the cottage.

"Hmmm," say some family members. "There's money to be made from this old shack."

"Don't be crazy," say other family members. "This is our cottage and it's always going to be our cottage."

Money, as usual, is shown to be the root of all evil. Actually, it's the love of money that is the root of all evil, as Timothy put it originally in 6:10. Either way, it can make cottage life a lot less warm and fuzzy for everyone, regardless of religious affiliation.

The fact is that there are people in every family who don't like the cottage all that much. It's never been a particularly advisable thing to say, so you don't hear it talked about, but you can tell by watching. They lack several of the talents that happy campers have. Here's a partial list:

1. The ability to use a hammer, saw, or axe

2. The willingness to sweat

3. The ability to withstand cold water, bugs, and downpours that come when there isn't an umbrella available

4. The ability to sit still without talking on a telephone

5. The ability to relax, to nap, to read a bad novel

6. Certain basic athletic skills, such as swimming and badminton and paddling a canoe

7. The ability to be a good sport when certain athletic skills are a lot more basic than the skills of others

8. The ability to take a joke

9. The ability to sacrifice a bit of privacy and a bit of individuality in a communal enterprise

Some people have more of these talents than others. Some have very few. For various reasons, many of them perfectly understandable, some people have never been good at cottaging and haven't enjoyed it all that much. But since the cottage was part of family history, family lore, and family tradition, there wasn't much they could do about it. Each summer they would go and be clumsy and not as happy as the others.

To make matters worse, their inadequacies would become part of the lore of the cottage. Every summer they would have to endure the jokes about not being able to hit a nail, about the time they fell out of or into the canoe, about the time they got lost on the path, fainted at the sight of blood, wore that ridiculous bathing suit, knocked over the badminton net, and spent half an hour trying to start the boat that time when they forgot to put it in neutral.

Worse still, they would have to smile and chuckle at it, because there's nothing worse than a bad sport.

When they grew up and formed families of their own, they found ways of spending as little time as possible at the cottage. The smart ones moved great distances away and sent heartfelt regrets every summer.

For those who stick around, however, resentments grow over the years. If everyone is having a great time at the cottage and you're not, you grow to dislike the place. In other walks of life, you can avoid having to do the things you are not good at. That is one of the privileges of being a grown-up. There is no avoiding it at the cottage. Grown up in all other ways, the unhappy cottager reverts to being a clumsy kid – yet another reason to secretly hate the place.

In the unluckiest of families, the discontent of the minority is not recognized by the majority. Worse, the discontented keep showing up, because they feel they have to. A clash between ecstasy and grouchiness takes place. The people who are loving every minute are annoyed at the people who are sulking. It ruins their fun. The people who are sulking are sulking, which is not really as enjoyable as it is cracked up to be.

Demographic events have an impact. The family grows. The children have children. There are divorces and remarriages and more children. All of a sudden, the place is not big enough anymore, especially on the weekends that everybody wants to be there. New tastes and habits are brought in by new family members. The old-timers want no part of them. The newcomers don't see why everything has to be done the old way. There are tensions, and eventually, some family members come to realize that they are actually finding reasons to avoid going.

Into this worsening atmosphere comes a financial event. A parent dies and the cottage is handed down and big taxes will have to be paid. A roof begins to leak and the cost of a new one will be high. The boat packs it in. A niece or nephew, the people who keep the place going, move to Saudi Arabia, taking their children. Above it looms the increasing awareness, encouraged by the classified ads, that the cottage – that building and acreage causing all this concern – would be really valuable to someone else.

To sell or not to sell?

"But it's been in our family for a century. It defines us."

"The roof leaks."

"But we owe it to our grandchildren to keep the place."

"The agent says we can get $856,000."

"Think of the badminton games."

"I am."

Thus does the cottage, that great uniter of families, become the great divider of families. Most families survive and most cottages do too. But when the great cottage murder mystery is written, you can bet that real estate will figure in the plot.

New Heroes of Cottage Country

Hungover on the Nature Walk

He agreed to do it because he was in a state of pre-guilt. Which is to say that he was having a good time, with way too much wine consumed and much more to be consumed yet, and he knew he would feel terrible and guilty tomorrow, so that when she proposed that he accompany her on the nature walk the next day, he weighed the pros and cons and said "Sure."

If he'd been sober, he never would have done it.

If he'd been sober, he never would have had to.

Now here he was in the woods, surrounded by elderly people, who were actually no more elderly than he, but seemed particularly elderly on this day because he was feeling elderly himself. The situation was not helped by the fact that they were all so cheerful, with their Tilley hats, long sleeves, and notebooks, their hiking boots, and water bottles cleverly attached to their waists on little belts. He had a water bottle but nothing to carry it with, other than his hand, and half of the water was gone already – and it was only water.

The sun was beginning to create a damp heat. And he was with people, enthusiastic people, who had all been looking forward to this day for a month, ever since the last walk, which had concentrated especially on mosses.

If he'd been sober the night before and not in a state of pre-guilt, he would have stated, quite impeccably, his reasons for not going. Why did you have to travel five kilometres by car to go for a walk in nature when nature surrounded you every minute of the day? he would have asked. Every time you stepped out the door was a nature walk. A walk to the outhouse was a nature walk. Under such circumstances, a nature walk was like getting on a bus from Newcastle to go look at coal in another town.

But it was he, wasn't it, who decided to open the next bottle of wine, even though no one else was demanding it. He had stepped off the moral high ground, corkscrew in hand. And look where it landed him.

It landed him along a path, mostly in the very bright sun, with flies buzzing around, in a group of chattering people walking really slowly. That was another thing: the hike was only three kilometres; with a good pace it could all be over in forty-five minutes or so, but these people walked so slowly. And kept stopping. And pointing at some plant, or often something that didn't even look like a plant and didn't sound like anything he had ever heard of, like a daisy or a water lily. A purple vetch, somebody said. Rhymes with retch, he immediately thought, on this day.

They would point out the plant and then stop and then talk about it. "Isn't that the same one we saw last month?"

"No, the one last month was less brown."

"What was it called?"

"Some kind of creeper."

"Georgia."

"No, Virginia."

Yes, Virginia, he was thinking. There is a purple vetch.

There was a group leader who, it was possible, might have had a hangover too, because he seemed to want to move along. But just when it appeared that the group might actually be achieving something resembling a stride, someone would stop him to make a point. Some brown-noser, trying to impress the leader. Amazing how you never get too old to be a brown-noser.

There may actually have been a plant called a brown-noser, or maybe he misheard. It was a plant that, according to someone, didn't necessarily climb trees. Some bird, or maybe it was an insect, buzzed around it, looking like a hummingbird, only it wasn't a hummingbird, because it lacked the humming-bird's distinctive something or other.

"Isn't this interesting," she said, falling in behind him.

"Very nice," he said. "Do you have any water left?"

It was impressive how she had educated herself, in the years since they'd been coming together to this part of the world, about the natural world around them. He knew the names of a few trees and, by repeating them constantly, had managed to convince the children that his knowledge extended ever further – although lately he'd noticed that they'd stopped asking him about anything other than the names of trees.

She, on the other hand, knew the mosses and grasses and wildflowers and had even picked up a little geology. She knew why there were no evergreens when there was limestone and granite, or why evergreens flourished with limestone and granite – whichever it was. It was only natural that she would want to share this knowledge and the joy that came from acquiring it.

But she'd picked the wrong man, a guy who generally liked the green look of things and the rocks and loons and whatnot but didn't feel an urge to learn too much about any of it. Instead, he liked watching golf on television, making a point of naming the trees beside the fairway if anyone looked at him like they thought he might have been wasting time. There were magnolias at Augusta; he remembered that.

On the overgrown track through the forest, he was notic-ing how large a noise a fly can make, how the sun can make you think you don't have sunglasses on, while he squinted at his watch, trying to calculate how much time remained before he could get into his car, turn up the air conditioning, and head home for a nap and seven glasses of water.

All he knew was that they hadn't turned around yet to head back when the argument erupted over the horsetails. The man with the CBC baseball cap claimed that the one on the other side of the track was a horsetail. The woman with the visor and zinc sunblock on her nose argued that this one here was a horsetail. The leader was nowhere in sight, and no one was going to move before he appeared to resolve the dispute.

It could make a person's head hurt.

When the leader finally arrived, having been detained seventy-five metres back on the path by a participant eager to learn more about bedstraw, he examined the two pretenders and declared them both to be horsetail. "They're both called horsetail," he said. "Only they're different plants."

Our hero sank slowly to the ground, pretending, once he got there, that he was merely tying a shoe. This is the meaning of life, he thought to himself. I come all this way, trudge at one kilometre per hour through a bug-infested forest, and what I learn is that no one knows which horsetail is which. At least with golf on TV, you know who wins.

No more drink, he pledged to himself – at least, not the night before nature walks.

The Cottage Industry

When the expression "cottage industry" was first uttered, it meant a family business – "*n.* a business activity partly or wholly carried on at home," according to Mr. Concise Oxford. We have a nice picture of the Joneses puttering about the house, happily taking pretty little statuettes out of the family kiln, the children painting them bright colours and putting them out for sale at the roadside stand.

Now the cottage itself is an industry, a billion-dollar operation supplying cottage owners with what they need and trying to convince them they need more. Not only boat manufacturers are involved, not only makers of insect repellent and chemical toilets, but all manner of designers, artisans, burglar-alarm manufacturers, mad scientists, and, yes, writers and publishers.

Although we think of the cottage as a timeless institution, although we think of time standing still at the cottage, time doesn't. Cottagers are as susceptible to new fads and changes in taste as any group of people. If you doubt it, think of the number of windsurfers you saw fifteen years ago and the number of windsurfers you saw this year. Now think of the number of kayaks you see today, as opposed to the number you saw fifteen years ago. The windsurfer goes, the kayak arrives. The only constant is that money changes hands. None of this comes cheap.

If anything symbolizes the economic power of the cottager, it is the success of the Canadian magazine *Cottage Life*. In an economic environment that swallows up magazines, new and old, *Cottage Life* has grown and prospered. Starting from nothing in 1988, *Cottage Life* now boasts a circulation of 70,000, which gives it, by the magic calculations magazines do, a readership of 1,140,000 readers per issue.

That's a lot of potential customers for the new BMW 5 Series with xDrive and the many other products advertised in the magazine. A quick run through a typical issue gives you an idea not only of the range of products available for cottagers, but also the advertisers' notions of what sort of people cottagers are. If you believe the advertisers, cottagers are interested in the following:

The Nikon digital camera

Cat food

Six kinds of things to float on from Canadian Tire, including one that looks like a daisy

Timbr, from TIM-BR Mart

A Royal Bank vacation property mortgage

A sign of our overindulgent times is seen in an ad for extra-wide boat seats. A sign of our importation of technology to the cottage is seen in the Dry Pack, which Canadian Tire boasts is "great for storing keys, GPS, cellphones, etc."

Because who would want to go out without their cellphone and GPS?

There's an inflatable water slide, a four-person inflatable boat, a VHF radio.

There's a pretty fancy car – an Infiniti – and several brands of SUVs.

There's the Honda Canadian Trail Edition TRX 500 Rubicon ATV, and you're not quite sure what that is, except that you suspect you don't much want it eating the trail where you're having your nature walk.

And yes, that other noise near the horizon is the Sea-Doo Utopia™ 205 Special Edition with all woodgrain details.

Star Choice has an ad for 100-per-cent-digital satellite TV: "Getting away from it all no longer means losing touch with what's happening in your world," it says. "Take the TV you love with you."

On the other hand, just to remind you that cottages are not only about ATVs, satellite television, Infinitis, and property mortgages are advertisements for the only all-in-one heart-worm, flea, and worm tablet, decks, insect bite treatment and prevention for the entire family, LePage sealant, lightning rods, barging, deerfly patches, croquet outfits, and, yes, hammocks.

The composite picture of the modern cottager that emerges from *Cottage Life*'s advertising pages is not one that varies too widely from what we would see in the city. The modern cottage has ceiling fans and all-weather, metal-clad wood windows available in ten designer colours. The modern cottager has things from IKEA but also Unilock paving stones and retaining walls to add "distinctive character and beauty to your retreat." The cottage may have nautical decor, and if it doesn't, that can be purchased.

Outside is a Ford Mustang, parked beside the animal-proof, weatherproof, do-it-yourself steel storage building, which houses the water purification equipment, pumps for water, pumps for trash, even – plus the $3,800 portable saw-mills for milling your own lumber. It might also be where you store your solar-powered marker buoy when you're not using it. And it might also be where you keep your garden supplies, your Moss-Gard to "prevent moss and lichens on roofs," and, in the off-season, the box containing your Dock in a Box, fea-turing Bird Deterrent.

Perhaps it's also where you keep your wireless remote control system for boat lifts.

Things are quite up to date on the culinary front as well. The modern cottage fridge contains flavoured bottled water. On the fridge door is a recipe for salad dressing, for those times "when dried herbs just won't do." When the modern cottager ventures out to eat, it is to McDonald's for a fruit-and-walnut salad.

The modern cottager's boat has drink holders, mounted with suction cups or stainless steel screws. It has cooler bags, a VHF radio, and a flare that looks like a revolver. On board is at least one tube of 100 per cent natural child- and pet-friendly outdoor lotion. In the modern cottager's tackle box is a reminder that fishing is now a contact sport – the Rapala Xtreme Action Slashbait: "The adrenaline pumping X-Rap slashbait has Xtreme attitude with its hard-cutting, aggressive darting action."

It sort of looks like the old Rapala, however.

The modern cottage is financed by Courage Capital. ("Want to spend more time at the cottage? Sell your business.") It has recreational residence insurance against theft, vandalism, snow load, and ice dam. It is protected by motorized shading and security shutters.

It may be a newly built custom home, it may be fractional cottage ownership starting at $84,900 ("breathtaking views, designer interiors, stone fireplaces, open concepts, three bedrooms, full furnishings, and total property management"). Or it may just be one of those old traditional cottages in a traditional cottage area like the one in the Muskoka/Parry Sound area with two hundred feet of sand beach and a mother-in-law suite for $1,149,000.

It could have many of the other items advertised in *Cottage Life*, such as tennis courts and basketball courts, the original do-it-yourself docking system, wind and solar generators, pine flooring, spiral stairs, sauna, teak furniture, hot tub, telescopes, binoculars and night-vision equipment, a gazebo, folk-art depictions of fish, an Invisible Fence for guaranteed pet containment, cottage antiques, vintage lighting, a telescoping flagpole, the Solar Sizzler for cooking "using only the energy of the sun," and your rather wide choice of toilet equipment. That would include composting toilets, some of which are "urine diverting," the Saniflo system, which enables you to "add a bathroom anywhere you want," and the PUU CEE insulated outhouse seat, fashioned out of Expanded PolyStyrene so that it "keeps your heat in and the cold away from you."

Down at the dock, the modern cottage would have the Safety Turtle, "the only safety device that instantly sounds an alarm if your child falls into the water." Floating nearby would be the Gator Guard, a thing that looks like an alligator and frightens away Canada geese, if not your child. On the bottom of the lake would be the noWEEDmat, "the only bottom barrier that respects the environment."

It goes without saying that the modern cottager cannot do everything herself or himself. Fortunately, an impressive service infrastructure has grown up around the cottage, giving the modern cottager access to:

Solar outfitters

Tree experts

"Eco Medic" shoreline restoration

Aquatic weed cutters

Boat restorers

Property maintenance service

Well drilling

On-site massage ("Natural pain and stress relief delivered to you")

If the modern Ontario cottager's email is down, he might be able to reach on-site massage therapists through the Surf Muskoka Cybercafé, although less privileged parts of the country might not be quite so connected.

Cottage country professionals may be needed to help the modern cottager install or learn to operate some of the essential features of the modern cottage. These would include the Water Weedsickle, which is "Transom mounted. Tips up like an outboard. . . . Self-sharpening. Self-lubricating."

Or it could be the Freeze Alarm, which telephones the modern cottager to warn about pipes freezing. "The Freeze

Alarm will automatically call three phone numbers if the temperature drops, power fails, or water is detected." It also connects to the cottage's heating system to turn up the heat before the cottagers arrive.

This, of course, presupposes a heating system, but that does not seem an outlandish supposition in this day and age.

The modern cottager might want to install advanced freeze protection for water pipes and roof de-icing, or a floating boathouse shelter, up to twenty-eight feet long, a new system to replace eavestroughs and downspouts, and tankless water heaters.

It is no small investment the modern cottager makes. No wonder the cottage has become such a serious business.

What to Talk about
at Dinner? Dinner.

One thing has certainly changed from your cottage childhood, and that is the amount of time spent thinking about, preparing, and, especially, talking about food.

It was not that long ago when all cottage food could be put into five categories:

1. Hamburger
2. Steak
3. Leftover steak
4. Macaroni and cheese
5. A fish that somebody caught, combined with leftover macaroni and cheese if the fish wasn't big enough

A rotation through that menu would pretty much fill up the week, with one day devoted to a picnic involving some kind of sandwich and another day eating french fries in town.

The preparation time was about what you'd expect, and the conversation about food consisted of the following:

"Is it hamburger today?"

"No, steak."

"Great."

That was the pre-meal conversation. The post-meal conversation went like this:

"Great hamburgers."

"Thanks."

There was no during-meal conversation, because of the difficulty of talking while eating a hamburger.

Another thing that distinguished dinner at the cottage in those days was the hour of it. It was at six o'clock and it was over at six-thirty. One reason for this was that you were a little kid, needed to be fed, and were likely to get all ratty if you had to wait for it too long. Another factor was the need to take advantage of the daylight after dinner (or supper, as it was called). If you wanted to fish or play ball or simply run around, you'd better get supper over with in a hurry.

The other thing was that supper wasn't exactly worth waiting for, in the sense that we think of it today.

The rationale for this particular diet was that this was the cottage. The cottage was not real life, so you didn't eat real-life foods, which consisted of roasts and casseroles and other dishes that needed better kitchen equipment than there was at the cottage. Cottages did not have electric ovens, microwaves, double sinks, and racks for hanging wineglasses from the ceiling.

That was another thing: no wine. Wine was expensive, heavy to carry, and why would you want to be all full of wine when you had to play badminton after supper? And why would you want to have wine with macaroni and cheese?

It was a simpler existence, in other words, which some people liked and other people obviously didn't. Check the recycling boxes at the marina to see if anybody drinks wine at the cottage now. Life has changed. For many, the cottage has now become synonymous with long, leisurely gourmet dinners, hours in the preparation and accompanied by fine wines.

Dinner will be at eight, perhaps later.

And conversation will be about dinner – the butcher store where this particular cut of meat was purchased, the spices that were rubbed into it, the special ingredients of the salad dressing, the best roadside stand for getting vegetables that were grown today, or perhaps picked today, whichever it is.

A typical pre-dinner conversation today:

"What time is dinner?"

"I don't know."

"Eight?"

Dinner lasts a long time and there is much to talk about. In addition to the ingredients, there are various dietary factors to discuss, such as calories, fat content, good cholesterol and bad cholesterol, and Omega something. At a large gathering, there will be several vegetarians of varying degrees of intensity and someone with an exotic allergy and someone who may or may not have an intolerance to something. There will be diets based on blood type versus those based on the phases of the moon. There will be those who insist on eating only locally grown ingredients and there will be those who wish that somebody local could grow a pineapple.

The elaborate food is made possible by the spread of elaborate kitchens in cottage country, and the availability of a greater range of foods and ingredients at stores in the area.

You can buy so many kinds of ocean fish at the store that no one would think of serving a caught fish, even if someone could catch one. Fishing is now done for prizes, rather than for eating.

A typical dinner table conversation:

"George caught a three-pound bass in the tournament last weekend."

"Congratulations, George. This is great salmon. Where did you buy it?"

As for the hamburger, should anyone deign to serve one, it can be made out of lamb, buffalo, elk, or veggie stuff, as well as beef of varying fat levels and varying resemblances to steak. This is progress: at last, hamburger worthy of being talked about at the dinner table (formerly the supper table).

All of this is a consequence of food becoming a more important part of our consciousness in the city. After real estate and perhaps hockey, food is the most frequent topic of conversation during the time in which food is consumed. During the hockey lockout, salad dressing briefly replaced the size of goal-tenders' equipment as the second most frequently discussed topic, according to the usual public opinion polls.

It is true that meals have always been a cottage preoccupation. When refrigeration and storage were not what they are now, it was necessary to plan meals, decide well in advance which night would be macaroni and which night would be steak, because of the need to shop. The shopping might not be done every day – in fact, it was one of the joys of cottage life that it might entail day after day of not shopping. Stores were less accessible, either by boat or by car, and there was not much in them, except for the stuff that kids liked.

Now the merchants in cottage towns have recognized where their multigrain bread is buttered. They make their stores into shrines to the gods of cuisine. The result is that dinner, which used to be something you got away from at the cottage, replacing it with supper, has been reborn. It takes up time, attention, and energy, and after it is over, there is little left.

Typical after-dinner conversation:

"That was nice."

"Right. Well, time to turn in. What time is breakfast?"

The emergence of dinner as a full-fledged cottage ritual disturbs those who want their cottage life to be less complicated than the one they escape from each summer. There is only a faint hope of that. It would involve our growing preoccupation with health taking the joy out of eating. People would get tired of spending so much time at it. They'd want to get it over with faster so that they could go catch a fish and eat it.

In the meantime, don't expect a lot of talk about anything other than meals at meals. There will also be a lot of talk about wine, which would bore the children silly, except that they will have already eaten – macaroni and cheese at six.

The Nap

Recognition Long Overdue

With all the ink studiously spilled in recent years over all aspects of cottage living, it is surprising that the nap has escaped scholarly attention. It is an important aspect of the lake life, one that helps distinguish it from the more inferior forms of living found in urban areas.

The cottage nap, when you think about it, is both a part of life and an escape from it. It is both a topic of conversation and an avoidance of it. It is sleep; it is even, on a particularly slow day, recreation. It enables the participant to maintain the will to carry on, at the same time as it enables the participant to avoid participating.

It is a pretty good thing.

As in all scholarly investigations, some definition of terms is necessary. The Urban Nap is the act of exhaustedly falling asleep. This happens because there is no alternative. The participant can't stay awake, although he (usually it is a he) tries. Thus, the Urban Nap typically takes place with the participant's head under a section of the newspaper. The participant is generally located lying down on a chesterfield or, in extreme circumstances, sitting up in a chair. In some common variations, the participant's television set is on, tuned to a sporting event. Golf is thought of as conducive to the Urban Nap, although the third NFL game of the day has also been shown to be effective.

In all circumstances, the participant's head rests at a peculiar angle, producing a stiff neck upon awakening.

Another common feature of the Urban Nap is denial. Upon awakening, the participant denies that he was sleeping. He was watching the game or, more commonly, thinking. The fact that his neck sits at an unusual angle is explained by some common city problem, such as a virus, air pollution, or "something in the salad."

All of these evasions can be explained by the fact that the nap is not considered acceptable activity in the city. It drains productivity. It takes time away from important pursuits such as going shopping for cheese. It is not pleasant to look at when a real estate agent is showing the house. For all of these reasons, the nap is undertaken furtively and, if detected, explained away guiltily with a canard about resting the eyes.

How tired the eyes get in the city.

The Cottage Nap, on the other hand, is guilt-free. It is considered a healthy and necessary activity, one that enables the cheerful mood of the participant. The nap is celebrated in cottage lore, and the napper is considered a contributor to our heritage.

Hence, the Cottage Nap is entered into deliberately, often even announced to fellow cottagers. "I'm going to have a little nap," the participant, either a man or a woman, might say.

In the city, such an announcement, were it to be made, would be greeted by words to the effect of "What about the cheese shopping?" This is why such announcements are never made in the city and why, instead, people accidentally fall asleep under the editorial page.

At the cottage, on the other hand, the usual response to "I'm going to have a little snooze" is "What a good idea!" or even "You deserve it." Thus encouraged, the participant heads cheerfully off to his or her bed for a sanctioned rest. Oddly, that rest is probably less needed than it is in the city, usually having been preceded only half a day earlier by a solid nine or ten hours' sleep.

This is yet another example of the embarrassment of riches that is cottage life.

Causality and methodology

Before this study proceeds further, it is necessary to establish some theories about causality. Why do cottagers nap? What purpose is served by it? Why is this activity so avidly pursued by cottagers?

The answers, as best they can be distilled from the available research, are as follows:

Why do people nap? *Because they can.*

What purpose is served by it? *Absolutely none.*

Why is this activity so avidly pursued? *Because we're groggy from the sun and had too much lunch.*

We can now proceed to some observations on methodology. One of the more interesting avenues to pursue is the relationship between napping and reading. Many nappers take a book with them as part of the napping ritual. The book is opened, a few words are read by the napper, who then puts the book aside and falls asleep.

Some researchers feel that the book functions, in this case, as a napping aid. The act of reading even a few lines slows the brain down sufficiently to make napping feasible.

Other scholars are of the opinion that the book is a napping crutch, symbolizing an extension of urban guilt. Conditioned by unfortunate city napping experiences, or even traumatic nap-related events in childhood, the cottage napper pretends, even to himself, that the activity to be entered upon is one other than actual napping.

Thus, rather than saying "I'm going to take a little nap," the napper says, "I think I'll go over and read," or, in some cases, "I'm just going to put my feet up for awhile." The first statement suggests that reading is a more worthwhile activity than napping. The second implies that there is something in the feet that will be improved by being put up.

In both cases, the participant is out like a light within minutes. When he or she awakens, an element of deniability is possible, if it is considered necessary. "I don't know what happened," the participant can claim. "I just put my feet up for a second, and next thing I knew, I was fast asleep."

This is denial again, but note here that cottage denial is quite different from city denial. The urban napper denies that he was asleep; the cottage napper only denies that she did it on purpose.

The sleep, once it happens, can be of varying duration. Some participants, conditioned by city napping, can no longer manage anything in excess of twenty minutes, which is the longest one can safely admit to in urban areas. Others, once they get into proper napping shape, can stretch it to an hour, or even two. (More than two hours is considered excessive even by cottage standards and precipitates remarks such as "Go see if there's anything wrong with your father.")

The twenty-minute nap has come under criticism recently, with opponents charging that it has become commodified. They point to articles in business publications that place an economic stamp of approval on the twenty-minute snooze, branding it a Power Nap, and associating it with various heroes of commerce. This, opponents maintain, makes the twenty-minute nap unsuitable for cottagers, who should be indulging in such an activity as napping only for the purest of reasons and not for any perceived benefit to the bottom line.

Devotees of the twenty-minute nap counter that it is an entirely untainted activity if you do it with your Winnipeg Blue Bombers T-shirt on. Of the nap itself, they say that they wake in an ungroggy state, unaware that they have napped, aware only that it is twenty minutes later than it was a minute ago. They can then pursue the rest of the day refreshed and without having to endure the taunts and skeptical glances that might have been directed at them had they been away longer.

Advocates of the hour-long nap maintain that it takes more than twenty minutes just to get a nap properly started and, further, that the hour they were unconscious was one in which nothing much was going on anyway, and they might have got sunburned if they'd stayed on the dock.

Two-hour nappers speak enthusiastically of the pleasure of awakening from a shorter nap *and then going back to sleep*. This more than compensates for the necessity to explain a two-hour absence. An experienced two-hour napper is distinguished by his or her ability to sleep easily for ten hours the same night. This ability is derived from years of practice and a clear conscience.

(Rookie cottagers often make the mistake of assuming that a two-hour nap is associated with sex. No serious napper would draw that conclusion, recognizing that the two activities, both worthy, need to be kept separate for full enjoyment.)

Great nappers of our time

As in any other forms of activity, certain accomplishments are celebrated above others. Wherever dedicated nappers gather, talk inevitably turns to those who have been able to execute the Rare Double.

The ability to execute the Rare Double (it is always "executed," by the way, never merely done) is usually reserved for more experienced nappers. Being able to execute the Rare Double takes the sting and some of the envy out of watching the young, fresh off their sleeping bags after a night of singing and worse beside some distant campfire, grabbing an orange juice and then heading right back to sleep on the couch before noon.

How many times have you said, "I wish I could do that"? Well, in fact, you can do something even better.

The Double harkens back to other daring feats of yore, an analogous one being that of the young acrobat Tony Curtis in the movie *Trapeze*, in which he, to impress the lovely Gina Lollobrigida, trained with the veteran catcher Burt Lancaster to bring off the Rare Triple – the triple in this case being a somersault in the air, rather than a nap on a mattress, but it's the same idea. As it happens, Burt became a catcher rather than a flyer, because he was injured trying to execute the Rare Triple, and couldn't fly any longer.

Considerably less risk attaches to those who attempt to execute the Rare Double nap, even without a net, but it is a significant accomplishment nonetheless, involving as it does the necessity of attaining full consciousness after the first part of the nap, this being accompanied by the ability to fend off feelings that it is necessary for some reason to get up. The classic Rare Double usually sees the participant rouse himself sufficiently to go back to his book, often located where he left it, on his chest, reading enough paragraphs to avoid disqualification, then going back to sleep again.

Upon awakening, he returns to the group with a spring in his step, one that can be easily misinterpreted but is recognized immediately by the cognoscenti.

"Did you . . . ?" they ask.

"Yup, the Double" is the reply, sometimes accompanied by a slapping of hands. It is yet another of those moments that make every cottage hardship worth the effort.

To answer the obvious question, yes, there are rumours of a Rare Triple being executed at a remote lake in northern Saskatchewan. Perhaps fearing that the acclaim and publicity might destroy the unspoiled quality of his life, the hero has not come forward. Perhaps this is just as well. It is still a feat others can dream about.

The New Rules for Cottage Guests (and the New Rules for Cottage Hosts)

Times have changed at the cottage and faster than you may have realized. There are new gizmos, new blights, new diseases, new perils of all sorts. All of these create both new pressures and new opportunities for cottage guests. There are more wrong things that can be done, more ways to avoid being invited back. That may be what you want, of course.

Early in the nineties, a list of rules I wrote for cottage guests was published in *Cottage Life* and subsequently republished in a book called *How to Be Not Too Bad*, a Canadian version of those ubiquitous guides to excellence. Most of the rules still apply, but progress has brought about a need for modifications. To refresh your memory, here are the old rules for cottage guests, juxtaposed with the new ones.

1. (The old rule) Don't expect your hosts to meet you on time. Their metabolism has slowed, and they have lost their sense of urgency.

1. **(The new rule) Don't phone from the car.** They went to the cottage to get away from people who phone from the car.

2. Do not feel it is necessary to show up in nautical gear.

2. Tilley hats are for amateurs. The proper cottage hat has an unfamiliar logo and grease stains, to show that you're prepared to get dirty. You can still hope that nobody takes you up on it.

3. Comment only favourably upon the cottage and its surroundings, avoiding words such as *quaint* and *cute*.

3. What you really want to know about the cottage is what it cost. You are not allowed to ask, although that information may well be volunteered. If the cottage is so modern it doesn't look like a cottage at all, don't say that. No matter how comfortable the cottage is, its occupants want to feel they are roughing it.

4. Do not feel that you have to comment upon everything, even favourably.

4. That lovely piece of driftwood may have cost several thousand dollars at a downtown gallery. Don't ask who dragged it in off the beach.

5. Normal rules of conversation apply: Dinner is not "grub"; a beer before dinner is not a "drinkie-poo."

5. Cottage food is often simpler and need not be analyzed in detail. The same goes for wine.

6. Dinner table conversation is about what happens at the cottage, not what happens at the office.

6. Never, under any circumstances, look at your BlackBerry when others are watching. Never, under any circumstances, talk about what you just saw when you looked.

7. Unless otherwise instructed, help with the dishes. Comments about the lack of a dishwasher are not helpful.

7. Just because dinner is over, doesn't mean you can turn on your cellphone. Don't forget to volunteer to empty the dishwasher.

8. Sex is permissible, but walls are thin.

8. Cottage bathrooms, if there are any, are communal. Govern yourself accordingly. Don't leave your Viagra on the counter.

9. The only answer to "How did you sleep?" is "Fine."

9. An equally relevant reply is that your back feels much better. You might be tempted to discuss what you've been working on at the gym, but avoid the temptation. If (see rule 10), you are reluctant to talk about your back, talk about what a fine day it looks like it will be. This, however, is not the time to talk about how your cellphone is so great that you can get the Weather Network on it and you know what the forecast is. Don't tell, unless you can make your forecast sound like you got it from looking at cloud formations and testing the wind with your finger.

10. Suss out quickly whether your hosts expect you to participate in work projects. Don't suggest any of your own (they may already have been done, only badly).

10. Too bad you mentioned how much better your back is feeling.

11. Avoid comparisons with the docks, boats, children, dogs, fish, canoes, and other features you have seen at other cottages.

11. That fascinating article you read in *Cottage Life* about the ideal septic system – keep it to yourself.

12. Size up the prevailing ethic – are you here for loud fun, quiet naps, reading, drinking, working? Then conform.

12. You may have to spend a weekend without high-speed Internet. Suck it up.

13. Try to interact peaceably and not judgmentally with the host's children, no matter what their chosen forms of activity.

13. This is not the time to discuss the new parenting philosophy you stumbled across on the Internet. Nor is it the time to apply it.

14. Be prepared to play games after dinner. Every cottage has them.

14. Two things: First, games that are on your cellphone don't count. Second, winning should not be too important to you at the cottage. However, if you want to win, go easy on the wine.

The rules for cottage hosts

Guests are not the only people with responsibilities at the cottage. Hosts also have the ability to ruin everything. There are rules for them too:

1. (The old rule) Stop bragging about the scenery. You didn't invent it.

1. (The new rule) Stop bragging about how you improved on the scenery. Some people liked that tree where it was.

2. You don't have to show guests photographs of the cottage. They are at it.

2. If your cottage doesn't have a website yet, don't worry. Your guests might find that refreshingly primitive.

3. Let guests know what the house rules are. Do you always flush? Do you *like* raccoons? Don't let your guests violate some unwritten rule and then laugh at them for it.

3. It's really important to warn guests that they are in for a vegetarian weekend, and that the kids are never told to wait.

4. Don't tease them about sleeping in if you didn't warn them that you get up early.

4. If you got up early to check your messages, spare your guests the details.

5. The rules of badminton and cribbage don't change, even though it's your cottage.

5. Video games at the cottage: an idea whose time still hasn't come.

6. Don't tell your guests how much fun other guests were.

6. That will all be covered on the website anyway.

7. Guests aren't afraid, on this special occasion, to overeat; don't be afraid, on this special occasion, to overfeed.

7. Judging by the passion with which people hold to their diets, food has become the new religion. In the interest of religious tolerance, find something else to talk about.

8. Don't apologize for the weather. Guests know it's not your fault, and they are willing to concede that it is always better than this.

8. Avoid the temptation to entertain your guests with recitations of the damage done by acid rain, zebra mussels, and whatever kind of moth is bothering you this year.

9. Guests don't need to know as much about the waste disposal system as you think they do.

9. Because of technological advances and the reliability of the power supply, it's not a bad idea to put that outhouse back up, just in case.

Who Wants to Go
to Town? Nobody?

When we were kids at the cottage, we always looked forward to going to town. Even if "town" was half a main street with two stores, a restaurant, and a gas station, we still wanted to go there. For one thing, town was different from the cottage. It was civilization. There was pavement there, stores, and people who were not our relatives. For another thing, we'd usually get a treat of some kind, a package of LifeSavers, at the very least, and maybe a new comic book. Some of us would look at the new fishing lures, others at the boats. Considering where we were coming from – a confined acreage with few diversions and overrun with relatives – town seemed like a pretty jumping place.

As we grew up a little bit, we might use the trip to town as an occasion to look at members of the opposite sex, maybe chat with them a bit, or at least wish we could have chatted with them. All of this added to the allure of town and made having to carry the groceries worth it.

Well, we've all changed and so has town. There are a lot more things going on there now, a greater variety of supplies available, and many more diversions. It isn't the same primitive place, where the screen door creaked when you entered the store and it was dark and smelled somehow of Kool-Aid. Town has changed, probably to correspond with our collective wishes, so we can't really complain.

Which isn't to say that we won't. As we do, we have to keep in mind that the town we romanticize in our memory of a cottage childhood may not really have existed. The store probably never smelled like Kool-Aid. The giant pike that lurked under the Main Street dock probably wasn't that big. The milkshakes may not have been the best in the world.

We should have recognized, even then, that there was something a bit deficient about the place. Otherwise, why would our parents have seen it as such a big ordeal to go in? Why, when we were jumping up and down demanding to be taken along, weren't they jumping up and down demanding to take us? Probably because they didn't see a whole lot to like there. And it's possible that if we, through the magic of a time machine, were returned as adults to the town of our childhood, we wouldn't be all that enthralled with it either.

On the other hand, look at what's replaced it. The best spot on the waterfront, the one where one of the five marinas used to be, before they were called marinas, is now the real estate office. The hardware store is an antique store. If you want hardware, you've got to go to the big mall on the outskirts of town. You can't get there in your boat. The outdoor store is there too, where the outdoors used to be, and if you get there by car you might lose your parking spot by the marina. The dairy is a pizza franchise. The bakery is another antique store. The pharmacy is still a pharmacy but now it doesn't have a soda fountain. Where the soda fountain was is an entire section devoted to scented candles.

The whole town seems to have been made over in the image of the tourists, a breed scorned by cottagers, who don't think of themselves as visitors, even though they are. It's just that they visit every year.

The tourists want scented candles, apparently, and T-shirts with pictures of giant smiling mosquitoes on them, and antiques and CDs of music with bubbling water sounds. Everything else has been moved to the mall, which you can't get to on foot either, a huge inconvenience to the cottagers who have arrived by boat. A steady stream of cars moves slowly along the main street. There is no evidence that any of them have ever stopped for anything, but somebody must have at some point.

Those who look for signs of improvement point to the fact that the old greasy spoons have been replaced, some of them by chain restaurants and some of them by attempts at haute cuisine that usually last half a summer, until the hard economic reality dawns on the owners: much as cottagers say they want gourmet food, they won't come in and sit down and pay for it, which they used to do for a grilled cheese sandwich or chicken fried rice. Still, now you can get interesting food, if you want it. Perhaps some day people will.

In the meantime, there is the roadhouse, which serves pizza, burgers, chicken, and the more familiar manifestations of Mexican cuisine. It has a patio and everybody goes there to drink beer outdoors and not listen to the music, the volume of which is controlled by a hard-of-hearing person.

Unlike the old town, which was there to serve the locals and the cottagers without making a fuss, the new town feels it has to entertain everybody. Perhaps this is because the town is in competition with other towns. Perhaps, again, it's a reflection of who we have become – people who can't entertain ourselves. Whatever the cause, the summer season has rock concerts and fishing derbies, both of which attract cars in large numbers and somehow cause congestion in the antique stores.

Who knew that fishermen liked chamomile bath salts?

There are also a number of large-scale events that are given the rather unmelodic suffix *fest*: Summerfest, Bassfest, Lakefest, August Long Weekendfest. More traffic infestations are caused by this.

In some cottage country towns that have more refined aspirations, summer theatre has arrived. It provides work for actors, which is good, and some of the plays are original and fun. The rest are warmed-over Agatha Christie and Neil Simon. Not surprisingly, this causes a run on the antique stores as well.

The latest growth industry in town is the literary festival. This causes a run on the liquor store. At the literary festival, authors descend upon the town in orthotic sandals and read from their works in the outdoors, trying hard to make their voices heard over the call of the loon and the amplified music from the roadhouse restaurant patio. Cottagers like the literary festival because it is something different to do, it makes them feel cultured, and it is cheap. Authors like the literary festival because it is something to do that is related to literature, unlike most of what they do. The literary festival validates them. Authors need validation, especially if their pay is low.

They do get paid a little bit, they can sell books, and, well, you never know. Something great could happen to an author at any given moment – like meeting a deep-pocketed publisher who has a cottage nearby. Or, better yet, finding a cottaging Hollywood producer who wants to film *At the Cottage*, with Robert De Niro and Gwyneth Paltrow. The notion that something great might happen at any moment is what allows authors to continue to be authors, despite everything.

At the very least, an author at a cottage literary festival might meet a Canadian metaphor, something that symbolizes all that we are and all that we were. Or perhaps the author might meet an actual bear. Picture the author then, slowly retreating, avoiding eye contact, thinking: What would Marian Engel do?

Needed: The rules for cottage towns

Life goes on in town, and what happens there doesn't always mirror what is happening on the lake. The full-time residents have needs, the tourists passing through have needs, the economic pressures that affect all towns affect the cottage town too. The mall opens on the outskirts of town. The local merchants close down and the chains move in. The young people move to the cities, except for the ones with the loud cars. The range of choice diminishes. There is one place to buy gas for the boat now instead of five.

It is not as if the townies love the summer people all that much either. Sure, they bring dollars with them, but they take up a lot of room. And they're always complaining about this and that, always wanting things done right away, always pointing out how much more choice there is in the city.

That's not how the cottagers see the relationship, of course. They see the rules always changing – about garbage and overnight parking and other things that matter. Each new summer it is necessary to do a crash course in how the town works. The grown-ups mutter with each new inconvenience, grumbling about what is being done with their tax dollars. The one thing that hasn't changed is that the kids always like to go there, because there are still LifeSavers.

Toward a Cottage Culture

Considering the number of humans who spend time at cottages and the number of historic days that they spend there, it's rather surprising that a vigorous cottage culture has failed to emerge. Think of it: where are the great cottage novels, plays, the great cottage movies, the great cottage pop songs?

Well, here's a cottage pop song:

Our little dream castle with every dream gone
Is lonely and silent – the shades are all drawn.
And my heart is heavy as I gaze upon
A cottage for sale.

The lawn we were proud of is waving in hay;
Our beautiful garden has withered away.
Where you planted roses, the weeds seem to say
A cottage for sale.

From every single window, I see your face.
But when I reach a window, there's empty space.
The key's in the mailbox the same as before.
But no one is waiting for me anymore.

The end of the story is told on the door:
A cottage for sale.

But that's not about the cottages we know, is it? "A Cottage for Sale" was written in 1930 and introduced by the composer Willard Robison and his Deep River Orchestra. Robison was from Alabama, not the Canadian Shield. The lyricist, Larry Conley, wasn't from cottage country either, you can tell.

"The lawn we were proud of" – what cottager has a lawn to be proud of? Even those who have them are more ashamed than anything.

"Where you planted roses" – no one plants roses. At worst, they put out potted petunias.

"The key's in the mailbox" – cottagers don't have mailboxes. They go to cottages to get away from mailboxes, not to mention keys.

The cottage in this song, made famous by the great Billy Eckstine, clearly comes from the British definition of a cottage, namely, "a house too small for English nobility to live in."

So the great cottage song has yet to be written. Perhaps it awaits a rhyme for *giardiasis* or *kayak*. It's true that elements of cottage living crop up in popular songs all the time. The moon is there. So is the shining water. So are clouds and trees. But the beaver is not sung about, nor the hornet's nest, nor the backache.

For the cottage in literature we can think of Margaret Atwood's *Surfacing*, published in Canada in 1972, which is awfully good on the emotional power of the wilderness. On the other hand, there's a lot about death in it, considerable symbolism, and a search for a missing father, not all of which are part of our usual summers. The cottages in Mordecai Richler's novels (*Barney's Version* and *Joshua Then and Now*) are rather grand establishments in Quebec's Eastern Townships, and the goings-on with the bear in Marian Engel's novel of the same name are not what we encounter in our routine cottage existence.

The problem is that when we think of cottage literature we think of the literature that we find at the cottage, which tends to be old Len Deighton novels that some visitor from the city left half-read. Time spent at the cottage equates, in our minds, with time spent getting away from all the city things, including thinking. Since we are getting away from thinking, we are getting away from serious reading. We are getting away from literature.

Hence the concept of the beach book – a lengthy, plot-heavy creation, easy on the symbolism, light on the motivation, heavy on the sex and violence. Knowing what the cottage reading audience wants, it's little wonder that serious cottage lit has not yet appeared.

So it's surprising then that we haven't yet seen The Great Cottage Mystery. It's a book with a natural readership, a book about people in hammocks to be read by people in hammocks. There is no shortage of plot lines, a wide range of possible victims and possible villains.

Cottage lit must, of necessity, reflect the thoughts, small as they are, that are going through people's heads as they travel life's journey at the cottage. Some titles with potential would include:

Great Solitaire Hands, in which a veteran cottage card player recounts times she almost didn't win, including that amazing sequence where the ace of diamonds turned up at just the right time, and that memorable occasion when she got the game that everybody learned from that visitor from Australia in one try.

The Wealthy Napper: A guide to creative investing that involves minimal reading of the financial pages and a large amount of time invested in the hammock.

Canoeing for Dummies: A guide to kayaking.

Paddle to the Sea Twice As Fast: The kayak version.

While we recognize the need for such titles, we still must recognize that there are dramatic events that befall us every summer, and why shouldn't they be immortalized in fiction?

Think of getting lost in the woods – not for very long, but still. Think of almost catching a huge, Hemingwayesque fish; think of that ominous noise you heard late one night, the drama of the annual canoe race, the time the barbecue caught fire, the bats flying through the living room. Now *there's* symbolism if you want it. Think of the memorable characters – your uncle who drinks, your other uncle who doesn't, the weird minister at the Li'l Chapel by the Bay, the hot guys at the marina, your grandfather who remembers the way it was, and it was really something, to hear him tell it. Think of the wild animals, the crazy storms, the bikinis.

You could make a great cottage movie, too, out of all that. Unfortunately, the cottage movie we think of most often is the one where Jane Fonda was in a bikini, *On Golden Pond*, and it's true that she fought with her father in that one, which is a good cottage theme. But cottages are not on ponds, except in Newfoundland, where some lakes are called that, and Jane and Henry certainly weren't in Newfoundland.

There are, to be sure, inherent problems in making The Great Cottage Movie. The movie would have to be done without car chases, an omission that many filmmakers find difficult. But there could be canoe chases. True, these last quite a while and cut into the time usually allotted to explosions. There could also be personal watercraft chases, but we already see those in TV dramas set at ocean beaches.

The trick may be to take some classic of cinema and adapt it to a cottage setting. Filmmakers are good at remaking old movies, which they do more frequently than making original ones. What about a cottage version of *Gone with the Wind*? Tara would be a large cottage, perhaps without the pillars, but with quite a big verandah. The person who plays Scarlett O'Hara could have quite a big verandah too, if the producers thought that necessary.

Instead of *Gone with the Wind*, the movie would be given a more appropriate title, such as *Not Bad Weather for Sailing*. Instead of the Civil War, the story would take place against the backdrop of a vicious twenty-first-century struggle in the courts over the zoning of a large lakefront property. Scarlett's relatives would go marching off to court. There couldn't be servants in this movie, because that would not be contemporary, but Scarlett's children could have a nanny, and there could be a role for the tennis pro at the yacht club.

Dialogue would be made more contemporary. Instead of saying "La-di-da," she would say "Whatever." And the Rhett Butler character, playing a casino manager who works for the provincial government, would say "Frankly, Scarlett, I don't give a crap." Only she wouldn't be called Scarlett. She would be given a more contemporary name, such as Madison. And Rhett, who would now be called Brent, would not say "Frankly." His speech would be modernized, so that now he would say:

"Make no mistake, Madison, I don't give a crap."

"Whatever, Brent."

This would be just before the sacking of the provincial campground by hordes of fanatical young men from a beer commercial.

Overwhelmed by emotion, Brent would look for stairs to carry Madison up. Not finding any, because Tara is a cottage, he would carry her out to the back deck, where they would watch the yacht club burning in the background, and she would say:

"Tomorrow is another August long weekend."

Putting tubing on the tube

The cottage drama has not really been tried on television either. There was a sitcom a few years ago, called *Mosquito Lake*, which was a promising start, but it didn't last long, perhaps because it was all shot indoors, for technical and economic reasons, thus depriving the viewer of sunsets and bikinis and footage of actual loons.

Such constraints still prevail, of course, and there is also the problem of many key TV elements not being present at the cottage. The mindless dad is around, to be sure, but overshopping, a key element in all sitcom plots, is not possible and a laugh track sounds even sillier than usual in the woods. Another problem is that a lot of cottage people don't watch television. Since many television stories concern people watching television, this cuts down even more on available plot lines.

Nevertheless, avenues exist for the creation of cottage-based television programming to enhance the cottage's contribution to the national culture. We have seen some of it already in magazine-type shows portraying cottage life at its most idyllic, heavy on the vintage wooden boats and barbecue recipes.

But there is new ground to explore, and the reality TV movement offers a path, one that should be taken soon before it fades out.

Survivor: The Cottage is the most obvious. We put sixteen good-looking young people at an island cottage with only the barest of essentials, including clothing, and see who gets voted off the island. The barest essentials would include only twelve beer, an outboard with just a 9.9 horsepower engine, two packages of (plain) potato chips each, some sunscreen with a very low SPF, no television or cellphones, and some of those old wicker chairs that lean even more when you sit on them. Although there are no crocodiles on the island, there are seagulls, mice, mosquitoes, wasps, and something heavy that goes "Mrrfff, mrrfff!" in the woods really late at night.

Then we see who survives. The resourceful contestants will search under the cottage for old comics to read. They will rescue crossword puzzles from discarded newspapers. All of this will be amazingly well lit, considering that they have officially left civilization.

They will find a pizza joint that delivers by boat. They will fall in love, which will be consummated mostly off-camera. They will plot against that self-centred one when she's off in the woods looking for salsa mix. They will compete at jigsaw puzzles showing Paris by Night and Green Gables by Day. Several corner pieces will be missing, and ominous music will be heard when that is learned. They will mutter about the guy whose hair always seems just a bit too neat. They will share those desolate, lonely moments that can happen to people abandoned in the wilderness with only a small camera crew.

There are other possibilities in the cottage reality area. A cottage makeover program could be a hit. So could a *Fear Factor* spinoff. There are many dangerous stunts to attempt at a cottage that could be adapted for attractive young people not wearing many clothes. And there are many nauseating things they could be forced to eat, many of which are handily available at the back of the fridge, where they've been since May 24.

The multigenerational character of the cottage environment offers many fruitful opportunities. Any skilful television producer can goad older cottagers into the kind of anger that shows up well on TV by asking them to offer their memories of important moments in cottage history. Since there are as many different versions of these events as there are people to relate them, and since each teller is convinced that the other tellers are dead wrong, they will soon be doing the kind of screaming at each other that is essential television viewing.

We mustn't forget also the potential offered by carefully edited selections from those old cottage videotapes people don't know what to do with but can't bear to throw out. With smartass voice-over and slapsticky music added, *America's Wackiest Cottage Videos* could be a hit. So could *Most Dangerous Cottage Weddings*.

Cottage art: The loon looks too much like a loon

Some of the other arts are on firmer ground at the cottage. Cottage painting (not painting the cottage, but painting the scenery) is, of course, in great shape, at least at a glance. Every cottage has a resident painter, and lakeside art galleries are springing up everywhere to exhibit their work – beautiful pictures of sunsets and clouds over the water, islands in the hazy distance, eagles circling, fish jumping, canoes silhouetted against the moon.

From an artistic point of view, there is a problem here, in that all cottage art looks like what it is about. The lakes look like lakes, the islands look like islands, the boats look like boats, and so forth. This is nice for hanging on the wall beside the stuffed pickerel, but it does nothing for artistic posterity.

Artistic posterity wants an unidentifiable swatch of colour that represents the artist's feelings about the sunset, rather than a representation of the sunset itself. Artistic posterity wants you to come into the gallery and say "What's that?" Artistic posterity wants you to think about the paintings rather than just look at them.

There is a need, in other words, to make cottage art less accessible, also maybe a bit darker and more ominous. We want a sense of the evil lurking behind the trees, the menace in the clouds, the peril under the sunset. Since few of us are able to think in those terms, it is little wonder that cottage art is in its present sorry state.

However, help is on the way. As cottages become more and more desirable from a real estate point of view, more and more people will buy cottages who don't really like them. The law of averages says that some of them will paint. You can count on their paintings reflecting the necessary pain.

The Sun Used to Be Your Friend

Twenty years ago, only visionaries and cranks recognized the evil qualities of the sun. They would go out in it rarely, and then sit muttering in shade, covered in clothing and a large shapeless hat.

Nowadays that description fits a lot of us, scared silly of the sun's properties. It's hard to ignore what we read, even if it goes against everything we were brought up to believe. We used to know that the sun was good for you. It would cure your colds, dry out your poison ivy, improve your mood, and above all, turn your skin an attractive darker shade.

Now we are told that isn't true. The sun is our enemy, all the more so because it is outwardly so attractive, a Jezebel, luring us out of doors when we should be indoors sorting cards to see if there is a deck that has fifty-two, plus jokers.

The more political of us will refuse to accept that this has always been true about the sun. If the sun is no longer our friend, it's because something or someone has turned it against us. There's that famous hole in the ozone layer. That could be it. The hole in the ozone layer was put there by all of us innocently spraying deodorant and hairspray around because we were persuaded to by the evil capitalists advertising on our TVs.

Comforting as that thought may be, the fact remains: the sun isn't as much of a friend as we once thought it was, and that realization has changed cottage life in significant ways.

For one thing, it has made people put on some really stupid-looking hats. For another, it has spawned a vast range of new products – do the capitalists have no shame? – alleged to protect us. Each year, the numbers on the sunscreens and sunblocks go higher and higher, an inevitable progression, mirroring the size of television screens. One year's 10 becomes last year's 30 and now people are wearing 40, and that's not as high as it goes. In happier days, the days of our parents' suntans, people put on something called suntan lotion, to *increase* the effect of the sun's rays.

Not everyone participates in the sunscreening – at the cottage, as in other walks of life, there are renegades – but now the non-participants get nagged, which is an unfortunate new development for them. Worse, elements of the style world have given support to the naggers by decreeing that pasty white is actually the most attractive shade for a white person to be. The tanned look is no longer to be desired, since it is either the product of an unhealthy lifestyle or the chemical representation of one.

However, opinion on this is not unanimous. Tan is still considered attractive by many people and magazines. And progress marches on, bringing a vast range of new products designed to get you that attractive darker shade without actually venturing out into the sun. Newspapers solemnly test them and announce the results. People must be buying and using the stuff.

The cottager has an unhappy choice: come back with a tan, which will cause you to be shunned or pitied by your friends, or come back wearing the same shade you left with, or perhaps a lighter one, which will have your friends asking when you're getting up to the cottage this year.

It's especially sad to think that we could have avoided all this by not spraying so much hairspray around.

Global warming: Not cool

The situation is not made any easier by the fact that the summer seems to have more sun, and the sun seems to have more heat. *Global warming* it is called, another example of bad progress, and everybody suffers from it, except for a few chief executives and think tank operatives who deny it from air-conditioned boardrooms.

Apparently we did this to ourselves too, with our air conditioners and the two cars we don't seem to be able to do without, what with the two jobs and you know how kids are so on the run these days.

So it's hot all the time, except when it's not. And when it's not, we get bigger winds than we've ever had, stronger rains, more dangerous thunderstorms, not to mention the hurricanes and flooding and tidal waves that are happening all over the world.

A little heat at the cottage is not so bad, since we can jump into the water whenever we want. Sleeping can be a problem, especially since air conditioning is still a long way in the future for most cottagers, thus postponing the irony of cottagers fighting global warming by contributing to it further.

Because most of us have a more traditional cottage mentality, we still think of cottage weather as being wildly variable, cold as well as hot. As a consequence, we make a point of bringing warm clothes each summer and then never wearing them. Since they are never worn, they sit in a trunk or a back closet, held for the cold weather of the following summer. With each summer, those clothes grow progressively unfashionable, another unpublicized consequence of global warming. Yes, global warming makes people dress badly. (If people only thought along those lines, the government would be given the political incentive to save the environment pretty darn quick.)

Eventually, the clothes are so out of date that they can only be worn in high winds, torrential rains, and tornadoes. Fortunately, these are now in greater supply.

What is bad about all this modern weather is that we don't really think of it as weather anymore. We don't talk about it the same way we used to talk about weather – in a tone of awe reflecting our belief that it was created by a force beyond our control. One of the great joys of getting to the lake was seeing weather up close, unfiltered by thick windows, unshielded by tall buildings – a great big storm, all around us, the lightning visible even through closed eyes, the remote but still real danger of something falling on us, the smell of the storm, the thrill of it, the relief of it being over.

What fun it was to talk about it afterwards. The storm would break the heat wave. It would be nice and fresh for a few days, good for sleeping, but it might be another hot one on the weekend. At the best kind of cottage, not much else is happening to talk about. There are few events, no agenda for the next day, no news, nothing on TV, ideally no TV. And since we have to talk about something, the weather has been it, almost by default, and because it is so interesting.

The weather conversation was democratic in a way few conversations are: the child's opinion was as good as her father's; the grandparent's view was in no way outdated; all could talk as equals. It used to be warmer, the summer of '46 especially. Remember last year when the big tree fell? I can remember when there was so much rain that the path was under a foot of water. Do you think the lightning last week was closer than the lightning that took down the big tree two years ago? And everyone could enjoy, once again, Uncle Phil's theories about the east wind.

Now we don't talk about the weather the same way. The sense of wonder is lacking, almost as if we don't really believe anymore that the weather is created by a force beyond our control. Now we are beginning to sense that at least some of this weather, the extreme part of it, is created by us. All of those things we did to the environment are coming back at us, and even when the result is a glorious hot day, perfect for lying on the dock and not getting a tan, we feel uneasy about it.

It feels unnatural, sort of like the tan we're going to get out of that bottle we just bought. Instead of enjoying our hot, cloudless day, we're thinking, "Damn, I should have skipped the hairspray."

At Last, The Great Cottage Mystery

Tensions run high at many cottages and one of the main sources of tension is whether to keep the place at all. Our villain could be a materialistic brother, Uncle Matt, in league with an evil real estate person, Stephanie Goldblazer, the two of them scheming to sell off the centuries-old family cottage to a company that builds spas on cottage property. The family, confronted with the possibility, is horrified to discover that the local authorities are in the developer's pocket and will approve the project. Yet to resist is hard, since back taxes are owing. The situation is desperate. Tempers flare.

When Uncle Matt's badly sunburned body is discovered, locked in an abandoned outhouse, Philo Evinrude, Cottage Detective, is summoned. He arrives in a small outboard, powered by an old twenty-horse engine that he keeps in spotless condition. He examines the crime scene and something puzzles him. The outhouse door was locked *from the inside*.

Philo also discovers at the scene of the crime an old Eaton's catalogue, dating from 1956, a happier time when Uncle Matt romped carefree in the woods and shot water pistols at chipmunks. Pages are missing. What does this mean, and how did Uncle Matt get a sunburn in the outhouse?

Could it be that the body was moved?

A wood stove, found abandoned in the forest, contains another clue – a love letter to the real estate agent from the minister of the Li'l Chapel by the Bay. In it, the minister refers to his excitement over the prospect of turning the chapel into a spa. He says many of the parishioners won't notice, and many will be happy to get a massage every Sunday during the offering.

Philo scratches his head, which has on it a Tilley Sherlock Holmes hat. Could the minister have murdered Uncle Matt in a fit of jealous rage over the collapse of his spa project? And is the minister sunburned?

Other questions remain to be answered. Uncle Matt's widow, Aunt Gillian, cancelled her regular tennis lesson on the day before her husband's body was discovered. Her alibi seems ironclad: she was dusting the cottage, and indeed it appears to have been dusted. Even the sailing trophies have been dusted, as well as the tricky part behind the canoe paddles that Uncle Matt hung on the living-room wall after the canoe was sold in the yacht club garage sale.

But Aunt Gillian has a sunburn.

A divorced cousin, Cecilia, seems attracted to Philo. She offers to show him her collection of vintage Archie Annuals. Thinking this might have something to do with the case, he accompanies her to a small cabin on the other side of the island, where she begins lighting candles in the middle of the afternoon. Telling her that he never mixes business with pleasure, Evinrude retreats with dignity, then takes a wrong turn on the path. He follows this new path, stopping when he hears angry voices. The grandfather, patriarch of the cottage, is arguing bitterly with his youngest son, Bill, about the condition of the pump. No one has put oil into it for weeks. "Mark my words, someone is going to get hurt," Grandfather says.

What does this mean? What grade of oil does the pump take? When Philo finally finds his way back to the cottage, he learns that, quite uncharacteristically, the children, Scott and Wendy, keep asking for sunscreen, although they refuse to go outside. Furthermore, potted plants that Cecilia has placed around the deck have disappeared, and graffiti have appeared on the personal watercraft.

Who would spray-paint a personal watercraft? Who would spray-paint the words "Death before disinheritance?" And on the other side, "Reggie loves Veronica"?

Philo Evinrude is not getting much help from the family. No one will talk about Grandfather's will. Did he leave everything to Uncle Matt? What's wrong with the pump anyway, and why is the dog afraid of squirrels? Cecilia, furious at being scorned, calls the police, alleging that Philo stole the priceless miniature birchbark canoe that her father bought for her years ago at a roadside place on Highway 17. A crusty Mountie arrives. He and Philo had a run-in a few years ago over the Case of the Disappearing Beaver Dam. The Mounties were about to arrest Philo's client until Philo was able to prove, by planting a bug on the clerk of the rural municipality, that the disappearance of the beaver dam was a simple case of rezoning.

The Mountie has not forgiven Philo for getting the better of him and is just about to lead him away in handcuffs when a fast boat pulls up at the dock and out steps Aunt Gillian, her face glowing, her nails manicured and painted. Surely, she wouldn't be visiting the spa on the day of the funeral!

"I suppose you're wondering why I've asked you to meet me here," Philo says, although he hasn't invited anyone, least of all the minister, who follows Aunt Gillian out of the boat, his nails manicured and painted.

Suddenly, there are loud noises from the cottage, where Stephanie Goldblazer is showing people around. Checking out the eaves, they have disturbed a nest of bats. They swarm about, the cottagers helpless to defend themselves, especially the ones whose nails have just been painted.

Philo remains at the dock. "I suppose you're wondering why I've asked you to meet me here," he repeats, a little more loudly. No one is meeting him there, and he is stunned at their rudeness.

"Back in the day," he muses to himself, "you could get people to stand still for the drawing-room scene. Why am I saying 'back in the day'? In the old days, I never said 'back in the day.' In the old days you could get a straight answer out of a cottager. Now they're so far into the white wine and moisturizers that they don't know which end is up. In the old days, I'd just light up a coffin nail and wait until someone confessed. Now I can't even smoke and no one confesses until they've sold the rights to the story. Also, you've got to muse a lot longer than you used to. A Cottage Detective's got it a lot harder these days."

He senses some motion in the bushes and finds Wendy and Scott, guilty looks on their faces. The dog, Flit, is with them too, its nails manicured and painted. Philo decides this is the time to draw his gun, but he doesn't have one, being a Canadian. All he has is a Cottage Detective's main weapon, a can of WD-40.

"One squeak out of you and I push the button," he says . . .

Bad Progress

Part 1: Something Happened to the Dark

The lake, these nights, is ablaze with light. In some ways, that's an improvement over the old lake, which was ablaze with nothing and you could run over a rock while searching for someone's dock, which was just over there, or maybe around the corner if you could only see the corner, which you could eventually after you ran up on it.

Now you can see the dock, because it has a big light on it. Plus, the house behind it is all floodlit. You just point your boat at the light and there you are. Another benefit is that if anybody wants to walk down to the dock in the middle of the night, he can find it. It may even be that the pathway to the dock is illuminated by those cute little solar lights that you stick into the ground. And if you stay at one of those extra-special cottages you see here and there, you may even find Christmas lights strung from the trees, yet another attempt to make nature look a little more interesting.

Once at the dock, gazing out over the dark water, you may be disappointed, however. One of the joys of the old, less-illuminated lake was the rare opportunity to be in total darkness – or at least a darkness that seemed to be total until your eyes adjusted and you noticed that there were 10 million stars,

most of them very bright, and also some lights moving across
the sky, high-flying airplanes, or even satellites and, on a good
August night, the odd shooting star.

On rare and wonderful occasions, the northern lights put
in an appearance, dancing across the sky in shifting patterns
and colours.

Critics of modern urban life often remark upon something
they call "light pollution" – the tendency of the city lights to
overpower the night sky. The cottage is an opportunity to get
away from all that, which is why it is doubly annoying to have
some guy's floodlight shining in your eye from across the lake
while you're trying to pick out constellations or watch for
shooting stars.

This once again pinpoints one of the major drawbacks of
modern technology, namely, our tendency to use it. The reason
we see so much light around the lake is that the lake is mostly
electrified. People have the lights on. But they turn them off
eventually, when they go to bed, which is when you wander
down to the dock to have a look at the night sky and discover
that lights are still on. Big strong ones.

Not only is the night sky taken away from us, but also that
delicious, if temporary, sense of aloneness that we can never
get anywhere else.

Can the darkness ever be returned to us? Not likely. The
only way it could happen is if governments decided to make
rules. The federal government won't do it, because it believes
that lights do not fall within federal jurisdiction (except maybe
at airports, and even there they may have been privatized).
This is entirely consistent, given the fact that the federal government spends much of its time trying to keep us in the dark.

Provincial governments, as we know, are in the pockets of
the powerful searchlight lobby. Which leaves local government. Local governments, as we also know, only make rules to
irritate us (such as by randomly shifting garbage collection
sites), and never make rules to please us (such as requiring that

personal watercraft only be operated in the winter months). So don't expect help from government at any level.

What we may be seeing is the arrival of a new type of cottager whose greatest fear is of being treated at the lake as he fears he will be treated in the city, not that he ever is. He fears that nefarious thugs and hooligans will attack his cottage, raid his wine cellar, pilfer his golf clubs and spray-paint graffiti on the personal watercraft.

As if the traditional cottage fears – bears, thunderstorms, bats, hornets, and that noise you just heard – were not enough, we now get urban angst.

Hence, the big lights. His protection from gangsters is your protection from darkness. Our only hope for the return of the darkness is the return of common sense. This has never actually happened.

Part 2: The Digital Cottage and Other Horrors

The cottage is not immune to the evils of consumerism. In fact, it may be less immune than other, less innocent aspects of life. This is because cottage country is booming and entrepreneurs are on the make. Entrepreneurs recognize that the cottage represents an idea of happiness and they know that happiness is something that people will spend for.

They will sell us a swimming pool, some of us, even though there is a lake right there. Next time you're in a plane flying over cottage country, count the number of swimming pools. There are not many of them, but there are some, more than there used to be, and why are they there?

They might be there because somebody always wanted a swimming pool, had the money to buy one, and temporarily forgot where he was. Or the pools might be there because those folks, having finally moved to a cottage, discovered that the water was too cold for them. Or the rocks under the water were difficult to walk on. Or there were weeds in the water off the dock. Or perhaps they were worried about germs in the water. Whatever the reason, the cottage swimming pool represents bad progress, of which there is no shortage.

Some of the bad progress is necessary. For example, the proliferation of bottled water represents bad progress. It is heavy to lug around, bulky to store, and it creates more garbage that has to be recycled. But it's there because the lake water isn't drinkable. If there were no bottled water, people would have to spend big money buying a filtering system. Or else they would have to drink soda pop and wine all the time, which is not as good an idea as it sounds. So there's no avoiding the bottled water, and the complaint is not with the bottled water itself but with the fact that it is needed.

Which is not to say that there are no potential excesses in the bottled-water world. Bottled water now has flavours. It has experts, connoisseurs who advocate one kind over another. In the city there are bars that specialize in types of water. As we have seen, the worst of city life finds a way of travelling down the highway to the cottage. So it is possible that the water itself could become more annoying than the fact that it's needed. When you hear about bottled water parties at your end of the lake, it's time to plan that city holiday you've been talking about.

The wary cottage consumer has to recognize that they will sell us anything, these guys, and they have enthusiastic accomplices in the mass media, who have difficulty recognizing what is new and what is not. Generations change in the newsrooms of the nation, so nothing is learned forever. Every hackneyed idea seems fresh to the next generation of journalists. That's too bad for you if you hoped you'd never have to read another article about that great new discovery, the diving board. You will, because new editors are born every day and each thinks that the public needs to know that, for example, playing cards is fun at the cottage.

Not only fun but, in the manner of all modern journalism, the hottest thing to do right now. There is always something that is the hottest thing to do right now. Well, no harm really. Being at the cottage is about ignoring dumb things in the paper and concentrating on the important things, like the puzzle, and reports on massive traffic tie-ups you missed.

But being at the cottage is also about harrumphing over the silly things they are doing these days, and it is with that in mind that you read what playing cards are selling for these days, the price of indulging in this newly hot summer activity. Let's see: Here's a set of cards especially made for playing Go Fish, only with these cards your kids also get to learn about art, because why play Go Fish if you're not educating yourself in some way, right? So while they collect sixes and jacks, they are also collecting Monets and Matisses. A deck of those costs $12.95.

There are limited-edition cards done by artists that cost $12.95 (the deck, not the card), there is a $10 deck that carries a Canadian geography lesson, there are cards with witty quotes, $11.95, and there are cards depicting various cocktails. Think of the family fun, eh, and don't forget to pick up another wilderness essential, the automatic card shuffler, battery powered, at $19.95.

The only solace to be found in this lies in the certainty that the decks will be, as decks always are at the cottage, mixed up, messed together into giant decks for playing rummy, and that a Van Gogh jack of diamonds will rest next to a brandy alexander jack of spades, next to a jack of hearts showing the seal of the Yukon Territory and a jack of clubs with a quote from Henry Kissinger. The lucky child will learn absolutely nothing from it, and the battery will be taken out of the card shuffler to make a flashlight work.

Part 3: Smile, You're a JPEG

And the first time the child, flashlight in hand, ventures down the path by himself at night, what should accompany him while he's by himself but a father, two aunts, and an older cousin, each one carrying a camera, each one determined to record this occasion for cottage posterity.

Cameras, like zebra mussels and purple loosestrife, have spread and multiplied in cottage country. This is not the worst example of bad progress to hit the landscape – the personal watercraft still rules – but it may be the most pervasive. No event is allowed to live on in memory alone. Whatever has happened, there will be a photograph of it.

Worse, it will be a digital photograph, which means it will be instantly available for viewing, which means that all activity will cease for the viewing of it. People stop shovelling to look at the back of the camera see how they look shovelling. People get up from the dock to view a photograph of them lying down on the dock. There are photos of cakes being baked, fish not being caught, people in boats, people in chairs, people chopping, napping, slapping mosquitoes, people laughing, smiling, and pretending to be laughing and smiling.

Because we stop everything to look at the pictures, we are put in the peculiar position of living our life vicariously at the same time as we are living it for real.

The prevalence of cameras also means that there is no private activity anymore. In the old days – which is to say fifteen years ago – the only people who had cameras were people who were serious about photography. Uncle Doug had his camera, a good one and quite complicated to operate. There were speeds and f-stops to calculate, and sometimes even filters. When the occasion arose upon which a photograph needed to be taken, someone would summon Uncle Doug, and he would do a proper job of it. If Uncle Doug wasn't around, the picture didn't get taken, which was often just as well.

Briefly, the videotape camera arrived, bringing a flood of action sequences with unrelated soundtracks and a lot of blurry motion, most of it from the camera moving. These were shown once on the family TV, put in a drawer, never looked at again, and eventually recorded over with the latest episode of *The Simpsons*. Video cameras were relatively bulky, complicated to use, and less interesting in their chronicling of events than our memories of those events. How could the tape of Junior swimming around the dock for the first time possibly compete with our memory, or Junior's memory, of swimming around the dock for the first time?

But photography exists mostly for the photographer, and the newest cameras are easier and more fun. So now everybody is a photographer. Many people, in fact, are nothing but photographers. It is impossible to get them to do the chores because they are too busy taking pictures of other people doing the chores.

So many people are photographers, in fact, that every photoworthy event has to be restaged several times, every significant grouping of people made to hold still while cameras are passed around so that every person in the vicinity can not only take a picture, but be in it as well.

In the ensuing months, those photographs, because they are digital, will be emailed all over the earth, clogging hard drives on several continents and confirming the suspicions of non-believers that one cottage looks pretty much like another. We know differently, of course, but the camera never lies – or at least people don't think that it does.

If there was a secret advantage to videotape, it was that it could not be emailed around, although it is rumoured that videotape can now be digitized, which sounds bad.

There is one unintended blessing in the new, digital technology, which is that not all of those photographs are printed and thereby allowed to clutter the drawers and flat surfaces of the cottage. Many of them stay in the camera and never emerge from it. When cameras are lost, as they inevitably are, the pictures are lost with them. There is no record of the meatless casserole being taken from the oven. There is no record of your ridiculous tennis outfit or the group photograph staged to commemorate something that looks exactly like the group photograph staged to commemorate something the year before.

Cameras get lost, and when that happens, sensitive cottagers know enough to look sympathetic.

New Heroes of Cottage Country

A Fisherperson at the Literary Festival

How did she get there? Well, actually it was pretty logical the way it happened. Weekend after weekend she was fishing. She fished in the early morning and came back too late for breakfast, and then she rushed everybody through an early dinner so that she could fish in the evening.

True, sometimes she took the grandchildren with her, which was several points in her favour, but she didn't do that often enough. What she really liked to do was just go off by herself in the little outboard, or even the canoe if the lake was calm enough, and fish, quietly, no one talking, no one asking questions. There was enough of that at the cottage.

Sometimes she brought fish back with her, and people seemed to appreciate that, and she cleaned and filleted them herself, which also should have been appreciated, but it took up a lot of room in the kitchen, always at a time when other people seemed to be busy in there and not everybody appreciated the look of fish guts.

Not everybody appreciated eating fish each time she caught one either. This was compounded by her resistance to allowing anything gourmet to happen to the fish. "You roll them in flour and cracker crumbs and fry them up," she always said, and that was that.

It wasn't easy being a woman who loved fishing. What would people call her? She liked "fisherman" herself, but people couldn't bring themselves to use the word. And it wasn't always easy to find other women to fish with.

Still, it was hard to stop fishing. Fishing grew on you, like an addiction. There was no moral high ground in fishing. It was much less harmful than a lot of those other addictions people have, but the fun you had from doing it all the time made it hard to refuse a reasonable suggestion, even when it didn't seem all that reasonable, like going to the literary festival.

"Just come once," he said. "You'll like it. There'll be famous authors there – well, maybe not famous, but published anyway, and one of them almost got shortlisted for something. One day they might be famous, and you can say you saw them when. Plus everybody we know will be there."

Of course, that was the reason to go fishing, so as not to see everyone she knew. But there was no choice.

They held the festival in the park in town, just beside the lake, and people brought their lawn chairs and floppy hats to keep off the sun. A woman she recognized from the town got up at the beginning and welcomed everybody to this, the third, or was it the fourth, Crappie Lake Literary Festival. Everyone applauded, which was about seventy-five of them. She was the president of the festival, and also the real estate agent, the fisherperson remembered, who showed their friends around a couple of years ago when they were thinking about a cottage on this lake.

Then the chairperson of this year's festival got up and said he had some housekeeping items to clear up right at the outset. First, there was no smoking at the festival, and anybody who needed to could go over there by the main dock. Second, while everybody appreciated a nice glass of wine, the festival's permit did not permit (and he chuckled over this pun, the permit and permit, then everybody else did too), did not permit the consumption of alcohol in the park. There would be a reception over at the restaurant (the Lakeside Gourmet, official restaurant of the festival) after each evening's final reading, and people could have a glass of wine over there and mingle with our authors.

Third, he had been asked to urge everyone to pick up their litter and deposit it in the litter containers, taking care to separate out the recyclable items, such as plastic water bottles.

Finally, no festival such as this one can exist without the support of its wonderful sponsors, so he urged everyone to consult their programs and patronize the sponsors who gave so generously to the festival or donated items, such as the folding chairs and the cheese that we'll all enjoy later.

The fisherperson consulted her program and saw that she would have to patronize the local funeral home, five tea rooms (two more had sprung up this year), plus a new roadhouse on the edge of town that featured non-stop exotic dancing. She would also have to patronize the city council, the member of Parliament from the Six Counties area, and a local maker of plastic pipe who, the fisherperson remembered, was married to the president.

The member of Parliament himself was there and was asked to say a few words. He said that the government, which he was pleased to belong to, vigorously supported culture and was particularly delighted to see this festival thriving in our thriving lakeside community. He knew how important literature was to our country and to the local economy. He thought he would conclude with a few appropriate words from Robert W. Service, and he did.

The chairperson introduced this evening's moderator, who was well known in the community and had been an active author himself for more than four years. Several of his short stories had been published in the local newspaper and one of them was a second runner-up in the regional short story competition.

"Did we come all this way to hear Dickie read one of his short stories?" the fisherperson whispered, a bit too loudly. "Maybe we could go to the Lakeside Gourmet now and get there before the cheese is all gone. Then we could mingle with him when he arrives."

Several people glared at her. It didn't help that she had not known how to dress for the event. She was wearing a faded pair of jeans and a T-shirt from the Toronto Blue Jays' last trip to the World Series, in 1993. Everybody else seemed to have on nicely pressed casual clothes of a type that she didn't think people wore to cottages. The lawn chair she had brought to sit on was old and much taller than those around her. She felt underdressed and oversized.

"He's just introducing the main speaker," her husband whispered. "We can get some cheese later. There will be lots."

"Will there be wine?"

"You don't even like wine."

"I might tonight."

The moderator said tonight's author needed no introduction. He introduced her for five minutes, mentioning the many books she had published, the short lists she had been on, the Canada Council travel grants she had received. He quoted from a favourable review she had received in an Australian newspaper and summarized the plot of her first novel. However, she wouldn't be reading from that one; she would be reading from another and I'm sure we're all looking forward to it.

The author was wearing black and appeared distracted. She said she had thought it would be appropriate to read from a book that was set in a town just like this one, but that seemed sort of obvious to her, so instead she was going to read from a book about sheepherders, which was set in Uruguay. Someone applauded this.

The mechanics of the reading did not go well. Although the sound system was perhaps stronger than it needed to be, it was of little help. When the author looked down at her text, her voice went off-microphone and people in the back had difficulty hearing. Being aware of that, she tried to recite from memory but stumbled frequently. The proceedings were interrupted several times by honking horns from young men driving slowly by who had apparently never seen a literary festival before.

The fisherperson looked at her watch – 7:25, at least another hour of daylight left. She scanned the lake and watched a young woman waterskiing, the boat racing past the park, with great whoops and applause in the boat for the skier.

Canada geese walked across the lawn, in the space separating the stage from the audience. This was just at the part where the older sheepherder was telling one of the younger sheepherders about his trip to Venezuela in 1973. The audience seemed transfixed. Several people took notes. The fisherperson knew them, having fished with them a couple of times. She looked over and winked, but they did not wink back.

She thought about pickerel, the way they hit the line so hard at the beginning, struggling mightily all the way to the boat, and about the way they tasted. She thought longingly about that stretch off an island she could see from here, where the boulders were and the big pickerel she had landed there in – well, actually, it might have been 1973 as well. Up on the stage, the author was reading from a part where the older sheepherder tells a different sheepherder about his trip to Venezuela, only this time the story is different from the one he told the first sheepherder.

"Huh?" the fisherperson said.

"Unreliable narrator," her husband whispered.

The fisherperson looked closely at the author and saw that there were five Post-it notes sticking out of her book, which meant she had three more passages to read. The first two had taken an average of twelve minutes each.

The fisherperson longed for cheese. She had never longed for cheese before.

After the reading was completed, which involved the story about the trip to Venezuela told from three other points of view, the fisherperson went to the Lakeside Gourmet for the reception. There was nothing to drink but warm white wine, no one to talk to about anything except literature. The author sat at a table signing books, a cluster of people around her, talking excitedly. The fisherperson ate some cheese and thought about bass, the way a big one jumps after it hits the line, then runs toward the boat, then jumps again, shaking its head and trying to spit the lure out. Someone asked her which panel discussion she was going to tomorrow. She said she had left her program in the park. What were the panel discussions about again?

Well, there was The Wilderness as a Metaphor in Canadian Literature. That was in the park where the reading was, only it would be in the church hall if it rained. There was the slide show about Venezuela. There was Rain Imagery over at the benches behind the town hall and there was How to Get Your Story Published – that was always the most popular one, and you had better sign up in advance because the library conference room could only hold forty people.

The fisherperson made her way back to the table where the warm wine was and talked to a man who, it turned out, would be the speaker at tomorrow's luncheon. He was an area writer, and, he said modestly, he had been on the back page of the *Globe and Mail* five times in the last three years. Two of those times were about the same illness, so he figured he must have a bit of a knack for writing. The second story was about the first anniversary of the first. The fisherperson thought longingly about being stranded in the middle of the lake with a motor that wouldn't start because fishing line was wrapped around the propeller.

The mayor walked by. She had fished with the mayor. The mayor said hello and wasn't this great. The fisherperson said it was different. If she wasn't doing this, she'd be doing the same thing she always did, which was fishing, so she supposed this was a good change. The mayor said it was great for the local economy. Well, maybe not great, but pretty darn good. The visiting authors stayed at local bed and breakfasts and ate lunch in local restaurants, and the people coming to the festival bought bottled water from various places, so it all added up.

"I bet you never thought, when you started coming to this lake, that some day we'd be having our own literary festival," the mayor said.

"That's true, I never thought that," the fisherperson replied.

Pest Update

Sorry about the Hummingbird Feeder

One of the many important aspects of cottage living that has changed is the pest situation. Sorry to report, to begin with, that there are more bears than before. They come up on the back deck. They wander into the kitchen in the off-season. They don't seem particularly frightened of us.

Why is that? It appears that it is because they feel quite at home. And the reason they feel quite at home is that they *are* quite at home. They are in their own neighbourhood. We happen to have moved into it.

Conventional wisdom is no good to us here. It says that bears will only come near civilization when they are desperate for food – in years of little rainfall when the berry crop is bad, for example. These are not conventional circumstances.

What is different in our circumstances is that we are moving farther and farther into the bush, finding new lakes, new trails, new places for subdivisions and golf courses. All of this puts us where the bears live. Think for a minute about your life as a black bear, the kind that show up in cottage country. One morning you wake up, crawl out of the cave, and come face to face with a gazebo – if a gazebo can be said to have a face, which you wouldn't really know one way or the other, since you are a bear. All you know is that something is there that wasn't there before. There are also smells that weren't there before. They smell like bacon and eggs and oranges – and was that sun-dried tomatoes?

Smells good anyway. Imagine someone being so kind as to bring all that nice stuff right to where you live. So you go to investigate and the next thing you know people are screaming and running, waving brooms at you, banging pots and pans, and yelling into telephones. Sheesh. You'd think *they* lived here.

Under normal circumstances, you'd do what you usually do, which is to give a little shrug and amble off into the bushes. But it's fun to listen to them debate whether they should play dead or not. Or should they run, or climb a tree, or stand their ground, or yell at you, or walk slowly backward, avoiding eye contact. And anyway, this is your turf, isn't it? So give it the little growl and, if you're feeling up to it, do the standing-on-the-hind-legs bit. Then you amble off into the bushes.

Later, though, when you're resting quietly, those smells come back to torment you. This time it smells like planked salmon and guacamole. You make a mental note to wander over later, maybe after the Michael Bublé CDs have stopped.

This scene is being repeated wherever people and wildlife meet, on the borders of their respective domains, with or without the guacamole. The frequency has increased because people (*a*) are moving farther and farther into bear country and (*b*) are less likely to shoot bears than they used to be.

Instead, they study the situation, learn the bear's likes and dislikes, and make a serious attempt to bearproof their properties, although refusing to consider the ultimate bearproofing of the property, which is to vacate it. Various commercial items are purchased, including garbage cans that people can't get into. The literature is scoured, and it reveals that compost heaps, so nice, so ecological, are not recommended. Nor are bird feeders, especially those nice hummingbird feeders. Bears routinely go after such devices, when guacamole is not available.

Understandably, some cottagers live a resentful existence, wrestling with garbage can lids, wishing for hummingbirds. But it's the price they pay. Some day, when cottage country has expanded almost as far as it can, they'll have to worry about polar bears.

Houseboats sail off into the sunset

Eventually, the bear situation will be brought under control. This could happen one of several ways. First, the bears could just get tired of the whole thing and move to the city, where there is already so much strange behaviour that they might not be noticed. Second, people could be intimidated and move their vacations to large hotels where uniformed staff prevent bears from taking the elevators. Third, the bears could lose the war with the hummingbirds. Fourth, people could begin bringing with them food that is completely unappetizing to bears. This is, in fact, already happening, with the unfortunate side effect that much of this food is unappetizing to humans as well. The bears, for their part, will go somewhere else, and return to a diet of berries. Humans do not have that option, although there is a chicken joint just down the road.

Other pests are losing ground as well. Partying house-boaters, once considered a peril by those within boom-box distance, have had their ranks thinned. This development is the result of the discovery that it's quite easy to fall down on one of those things, particularly in a wind, and that the fall from top to bottom is painful. It has been further discovered that if your arm is in a cast, it's very difficult to open a beer bottle. House-boats are mostly inhabited now by people who know what they are doing and have no ambition to broadcast music to the entire lake.

As a nuisance, they have now been replaced by people who use their boats as cottages. Huge boats they are, which moor together wherever there is an unoccupied bay. These boats are suitable for ocean voyages and have more space in them than many cottages, and more gadgets. Being able to take the cottage with you is one cure for the difficulty of acquiring land – although one could easily afford to acquire the land by selling the boat. To see a dozen of them huddled together in a sheltered spot is to be reminded of a trailer park – a trailer park for millionaires.

Their music won't be played loud enough to bother you, though you might tire a bit of *The Big Chill* soundtrack.

They, like another perennial nuisance, the personal watercrafters, might eventually be taken from us by the high price of gasoline. An extra disincentive for personal watercrafters is that they will begin to hate noise as they grow older, and also realize that they look really dumb.

A sure cure for foodies

As to other pests, it is true that raccoons remain in some jurisdictions, and golfers are proliferating in others, but the mosquitoes are being vacuumed up by some gadget purchased in the chapter "The Cottage Industry." Weeds are being hacked away with powerful underwater blades or trampled down by underwater mats. That noisy bird has fled, tired of assaults on its privacy by kayak-borne paparazzi.

Flies remain, one of the few cottage pests that has no human support group. There is no National Council for the Protection of Flies. Ever notice that? Despite this rare unanimity about their unworthiness to share the planet with us, flies are not easy to eradicate. All that can be usefully said is that they are here for a while, and then they are gone. This is comforting only when they are gone.

In the good old days, the days of the Founding Cottagers, flypaper, hung strategically from the ceiling and, at the end of the day, was covered with stuck and dead flies. For some reason, that habit has gone out of practice, with today's cottager considering it a fashion crime to have a cottage ceiling covered in dead flies. There is no accounting for taste. Anyway, in most seasons, flies are out of season.

That leaves . . . what? Well, foodies, long a nuisance in the city, are now expanding their operations. You can kill a fly by hanging sticky paper from the ceiling. It's more difficult to know what to do about the guy who brings his personal salad dressing everywhere he goes, two or three bottles each time and to so many cottages that cutting back the supply by regifting is out of the question. Only in recent years have men learned how to make salad dressing, and it is one of the difficulties that could not have been envisioned by the Founding Cottagers. It is yet another reminder that a cottager can't become complacent, that new pests are continuously being invented and, indeed, born.

But salad dressing is, after all, only salad dressing. Surely we can overcome it.

It's possible, for example, that a more sophisticated, high-tech version of flypaper can be invented for use against those who refuse to talk about the weather, refuse to discuss the sailing trophies on the wall, the poison ivy this year, the new dock, Juliana's new tooth, and the cute way the dog cocks his head whenever a loon calls – refuse to discuss these things because they want to talk about the way the veal is done or the place in Vancouver where they had the exquisite sea bass last April.

The question remains what you do with such a person once he is stuck to the paper. You can't just throw him out. He's your guest. Anyway, the recycling depot won't accept him.

Americans, tourists, and bats

In *At the Cottage* there was a detailed list of cottage pests. These included, as well as some of those listed above, bats, friends, fiancés, tourists, and Americans. Most of those remain with us, although some at a reduced level. Americans fit into this category, worried about their dollar, about catching some disease they heard on CNN we have up here, maybe something about cows. Those who do risk a visit are sensitive to the point of obsequiousness, so nervous are they about being yelled at for the foreign-policy sins of their administration.

As before, that loud-talking, obnoxious guy making un-reasonable demands in restaurants is likely to be one of ours.

The tourists are as before too. The towns serving cottage country have shifted their economic base in such a way as to be even more responsive to tourists' needs. That means that there are more stores that sell scented candles, T-shirts with pictures of smiling moose on them, and CDs of New Age music that is supposed to sound like the seashore. Conversely, there are fewer stores that have a sufficient variety of insect repellents and galvanized nails. Not much can be done about that, particularly since cottagers now make a habit of stocking up on such items in the city before leaving. That further diminishes any economic clout the cottagers might have. As always, none of this is the poor tourist's fault. He just wants to pick up his bag of salt-and-vinegar chips and some drinks for the kids and get back on the road. It probably puzzles him as much as anyone that he can't seem to buy anything that's actually made here.

As for the bats, they are still there, but probably much more appreciated than they were, partly for their willingness to eat mosquitoes, a sacrifice few others of us are prepared to make – and partly also because they are genuinely wild things with the capacity to frighten us a little bit.

The bat's place in the annals of cottage menace might have been supplanted by the Canada goose, which looks magnificent in flight but appears clumsy on the ground, where it also has a habit of excreting at a world-record volume (assuming that they keep world records of these things, which they probably do).

Those who hate golf have a grudging affection for the Canada goose, for its prolific decorating of golf courses. This, the antigolfers hope, will, in the end, save vanishing farmland, but it seems a vain hope. Most Canadians still thrill to the sight of the geese flying overhead in formation, but hope, without really admitting it to anyone, that they will land somewhere else.

For that matter, the Canada goose isn't even the national symbol, which of course is the beaver. The beaver, to its growing list of enemies, resembles the Canada goose in that it looks its best in the distance, heading the other way. But he may just have come from taking down one of your nicest trees. And the beaver is a pretty fair excreter himself, as you will know if one has ever paused on your dock.

It is no surprise, then, that a serious attempt is now being made to declare the beaver a pest. This must be vigorously opposed. While it is technically true that Canada's national symbol chews down trees, some of them quite nice ones, and leaves them lying in inconvenient places, such as across the top of the old cabin, the national symbol is only doing what it was intended to do by nature, so that's where you should direct your complaints. Trapping beavers, which some cottagers advocate, would be marginally acceptable if the cottagers were needy folk in search of pelts. But that is not the case. The beavers are more needy than the cottagers. The beavers need tree bark to eat and little branches to make their houses with. We, who need neither of those things, should have a bit more sympathy. If the beaver goes, so does that lovely sight, beloved of cottagers through the generations, of the beaver swimming softly across the lake, dragging a little branch into the sunset, then banging its tail on the water when it senses it is threatened with having its picture taken.

Canadians have grown pretty angry at beavers in recent years. This could be the result of a contempt for our national symbolism, brought about by the right-wing media, or it could be the result of a contempt for fallen trees, brought about by fallen trees. Occasionally, we have to remember that the beaver was here before we were, and the beaver does what beavers do, which is to cut down trees, build dams, and drag branches serenely through the water at sunset. And we do what we do, which is spray chemicals around, spill things in the lake, make loud noises with machines, and curse at fallen trees.

Think what a pest we are to the other creatures.

We have met the enemy

And that pretty much sums it up. The biggest cottage pest is us. Certainly there is room for debate as to which of us are bigger pests than others. Is it young people, old people, stick-in-the-muds who oppose change, developers who push change, golfers, partyers, property owners – you can find just about anyone to blame.

In fact, there is a theory, which you can accept or not, depending on your degree of innate conservatism, that the real cottage pest these days is government. You can often hear someone expound this theory just after having been denied permission to do something perfectly reasonable, like put up a three-storey boathouse with two bathrooms just overhanging the lake a little bit.

You might begin to feel that way yourself some day when you're off on a nice little boat excursion and find a sign limiting you to ten kilometres per hour. It is just slow enough to keep you from planing, just fast enough for you to create a wake that will swamp any canoeists who happen to be in the vicinity, and you know, just know, that the number ten was arrived at by a group of bureaucrats in a meeting room at least ten kilometres from the nearest water.

True, it is a slight improvement, in the logical sense, over the nine miles per hour that used to decorate narrow and high-traffic sections of the lake, the only reasonable explanation for the nine being that it was somebody's favourite number.

Now, you wouldn't mind so much if you knew that government was on the scene there grabbing the people going eleven, or, more to the point, forty-one, but that doesn't seem to be government's style. Government puts up the signs, and everything else is pretty much up to you.

It's government telling you to slow down and by how much. It's government telling you you have to have a whistle in your canoe, and how many life preservers you have to keep in your boat, and that you have to have a fishing licence even if you only catch two a year, and that's if you're lucky. It's government that says you can't put up a new building even if you tear down the old one, but you can add to the old one to such an extent that it might as well be new.

It's government that tells you when you can have a fire and what you can't put out in your garbage this year and what the hell are you supposed to do with it if you can't put it out?

Oh right, and don't forget that it's government that decides that the long weekend is the perfect time to rebuild that bridge on the highway everybody has to take to get up here.

It's also government that doesn't do anything about the noise coming from across the lake, all that loud music, and were those gunshots?

The way we all look at it – and it seems perfectly logical from the vantage point of a slightly tilting chair on the dock – is that if government does it, it's too much and if government doesn't do it, it's too little. Or is that us that's slightly tilting?

Mosquitoes never had to endure the criticism that government gets. Mind you, one slap and the mosquito is history, which is more than you can say for government.

Where government may have overstepped this time is with these boater tests. The idea isn't all that bad on the surface – make sure nine-year-olds know what they're doing before they get their hands on the throttle, or wherever their hands go. You can see that they should know which way is port and which is starboard, even if their parents never did, which is the bow and which is the stern, whether to go left or right of the green, and what to do when there is a sailboat in the way.

It's good they should know all those things, since they're just starting out. But us? Hey, we know all that, at least the important parts of it. If we don't know port and starboard, we at least know right and left, or is it left and right? When, while driving at night, we see a boat ahead of us showing a green light, we know that it's either coming toward us or going away. And we know that you should always wave at boats as they go by and put lots of those floating cushions in the boat if there aren't life preservers, and one of these days we're going to find out whether those floating seat cushions are legal anymore.

Aside from that, what's there to know?

Endless Twilight

One of the most significant changes in the life of the cottage is demographic. The population of North America is getting older and so is the population at the cottage. A goodly number of those baby boomers who have been driving the economy and the culture for so long are looking at sixty. Many of them are looking at retirement. Many of them are looking to spend more days at the lake, and it is becoming much easier for them to do so.

Obsessed as we are by bad progress, we shouldn't overlook how much has been done to make life easier for older people at the cottage. There are decks and ramps and lifts and rails. There are telephones, just in case. There are better shoes with a better grip, to help in the survival of those moments when the path is not as it was. Boats are easier to get into and out of, more sheltered from the elements. There is better lighting. There are toilet advances, which is perhaps an odd way to put it. There are more puzzles in the newspaper, which is available earlier in the day. There are hats that don't make you look like an absolute idiot when a loved one forces you to put one on. There are better kitchens, better able to produce the kinds of food that agree with older digestive systems.

All of which means that there will be more old people at the cottage. This is an entirely good thing, but it poses some challenges. For one, people become more set in their ways as they become older. That means they defend good traditions and it means they defend bad ones. It means that they prevent a cherished old blanket from being thrown out because they know the crucial role it played just after the war when that near tragedy happened at the picnic down the lake. On the other hand, the place would operate a lot better if we could get rid of some of the junk that's been accumulating for seventy-five years.

Another challenge is adjusting the place to people who move less easily and won't always be in the best of health. That can cost money – putting in the extra bathroom – or it can take up space – declaring certain areas off limits to children at certain hours. It can mean making paths and docks more walkable. It can mean knowing where the nearest doctor is. It can mean letting Grandma have first crack at the crossword.

Or it can mean just speaking up.

It has to be remembered that sixty-year-olds do not consider themselves old, and many of them won't behave that way. Nor will sixty-five-year-olds, although some may have to. Seventy-year-olds are not old either, if you ask them. But somehow, despite the fact that none of these people are old, the cottage will become an older place.

That's a good thing, because old people – let's call them old, for the sake of something to call them – bring much that is valuable to the cottage. That doesn't just mean babysitting – although there is no denying the value of that.

Old people bring a link with earlier days, a memory, sometimes enhanced, of what things were like before all this. They know who used to live on the little island out in the channel and how they got their comeuppance. They remember what the point looked like before the trees grew up. They remember the biggest fish, the strongest wind, the owners of the bakery where the Canadian Tire is now. They remember the best places to hide. They remember the embarrassing incident at the dinner table when the minister dropped by unexpectedly.

So much of cottage conversation is lore, much of it, though not all, provided by the older people. When they go, it is passed on by the next generation, retaining not all of it and probably reshaping it a bit, plus adding some of their own memories, when those memories have moved far enough into the past to become lore as well. Another important aspect of lore is that passed on by the youngest, comprising their vivid memories of what happened on this exact spot on the dock last year. It may have been an incident involving a spider and the thing you said, which you have completely forgotten but which they remember word for word.

The old people are counted upon for their cottageman-ship – that is, their knowledge of how the pump works, what to do with an axe in a certain situation, the exact procedure for dealing with mice. They may not, in fact, know, but the best cottage old people are never reluctant to make something up, which may then find itself in cottage lore as the years go by. Somebody looks up from putting peanut butter on the mouse-trap and wonders out loud why, and the answer may have been a total bluff that an old person got away with forty years ago.

The old people are also a useful bulwark against bad progress. Bad progress, bit by bit, makes the cottage more noisy, makes the cottage experience more and more like the city expe-rience, makes the lake less neighbourly. Old people don't like that. They think that if they can dig in their heels long enough, their children will become old enough not to like it either.

The digging in of heels takes many forms. One of them is the questioning of cost. The last time most old people bought anything for themselves, it cost about one third of what it does now. Since everything seems expensive to them, they will react in horror to the price tag of each shiny gadget. "Can we really afford it?" they will ask. And they will add the telling comment that "We got along without it just fine." That's quite a powerful argument when you think about it, and the only one that trumps it is "Times have changed, Dad." Wise sons and daughters save that one for when it is absolutely necessary.

One of the most valuable qualities old people bring to the cottage is an aversion to noise. Why that is, is difficult to say. It is not that old people grew up hating noise. The older baby boomers turned up the volume on their Beatles records. The generation even older than that had their Elvis 45s playing as loud as they would go. They liked loud cars and loud parties. But now they are older, and even though they don't hear as well, noise bothers them. That suits the cottage environment just fine. Most of the folks at the lake are there to escape noise. The old people are their leaders and their inspiration and their occasional nags. Together, they make the lake a quieter place.

Old people are also antigadget. Again, it's difficult to know why this is. The people who are old now grew up with gadgets, such as the Pocket Fisherman, the hula hoop, and whipped cream you sprayed out of a can. But at a certain point in their lives, a little light flashes, a buzzer sounds, and a sign illuminates in the mind. "ENOUGH GADGETS," it says. From that point on, the old person decrees, if he can, that no more gadgets are needed, and the cottage will have to make do with what it has now.

Find a cottage without a leaf blower, a personal watercraft, battery-operated corkscrew, a garage, a flat-screen TV, or even a non-flat-screen TV, and you will know that there is an old person there who is still listened to, at least some of the time.

It has to be noted that old people can be bulwarks against good progress as well. It actually doesn't matter what kind of progress it is, old people can be bulwarks against it. That is why the smarter ones conserve their powers and pick their spots. Keeping the leaf blower off the island was probably worth the effort. But that turtle-shaped thing that the kids throw around the dock – keeping it off the island was probably not all that necessary.

In the end the old people won't halt either kind of progress. But they can at least force the progressives to stop and think and to justify what they are doing, before investing valuable funds in a helicopter pad or a website. Investing in boardwalks, handrails, and a lamp you can actually read by – well, that's another story.

Something Happened to the Quiet

One of the great unsung cottage occasions of the year is Labour Day night. If you are lucky enough not to have gone home yet, you will know what that means. Around sunset, you stand on the dock and listen, and hear nothing, except the distant hum of cars on the highway, heading back to the city. All the people have gone, and they have taken with them their dogs and children and power tools and audio equipment. They have put the personal watercraft in the boathouse, along with the boat. Nothing is moving on the lake, except some loons and heron.

If you are far enough from the highway, you don't even hear the hum of distant traffic. You've been longing for quiet all summer, and here it is.

True, summer is mostly gone, but still . . .

If you have ever been lucky enough to be able to stay for the next day or week or two, you remember what comes next – days of glorious peace, glorious calm, a wonderful sense of aloneness, a feeling, however unrealistic, that you are close to nature, isolated. The leaves begin to change, bit by bit, giving the lake a look you've never seen. You feel, when you venture out, alone, that there is nobody but you and the animals, and that they are watching you.

That's the kind of delicious paranoia you can develop when you are all by yourself at the cottage after Labour Day. And even if you can, through the wonders of electricity, go inside and turn on the lights, that feeling of smallness, of your insignificance in the outdoors, persists. If you can't turn on the lights, if you are living by flashlight and wood stove, the feeling is that much greater.

It is probably the feeling that your grandfather and grandmother had most of the time. These days it is hard to find, until the second week in September.

Aaaahhh. The Jet Skis are gone, the neighbours yelling at their children are gone, the dog that barks when it is left alone, as it always is, and your own relatives that you love dearly but they do like to chat sometimes. It's just you and the . . . and the what? Well, the noise of construction across the lake. The jackhammers and chainsaws and generators and cement mixers. They've started. There are more of them than ever, more than at midsummer.

And why? Because people around the lake have improvements they want to make, and they can't make them themselves. Making the improvements, building that gazebo they saw in the magazine, would take time and energy and cause saws to sound and nails to be hammered while people are trying to sleep in the summertime. Better to let it wait and hire someone to do it after Labour Day.

So that's what the sound is. Your neighbour's new gazebo being constructed on a clear, crisp, and otherwise soundless September day. Across the lake, there's a chainsaw sound. That would be the guys hired by the Joneses to take down some trees to accommodate the planting of a lawn. The guys have lots of time to work in the fall, with everybody gone back after the summer. Next door is the expansion of the Walker place, the new wing. Looks like they're getting ready to make it into their permanent residence.

You hear some banging that sounds like rocks being crushed, an explosion that is the dynamiting of a stump. You hear trucks and backing-up beeping.

The lake has become a construction site. The noise is bad enough, but what it represents is worse. It means that people are moving in permanently. There will always be somebody at the lake now. You'll never have it to yourself again.

Oh well. It was great while it lasted.

Part 2

Cottage Country Enters the Future,
Somewhat Reluctantly

Could It Possibly Get Any Better? Perhaps Just a Bit.

Let us now consider the cottage of the future. Scan ahead to, say, 2050 and look around you.

Isn't it beautiful? The sky is a nice clear blue. The same great rocks are there, and the white pines are even taller. The water is clear and unpolluted. Boat traffic moves nicely along, but not too fast, and the motors are so quiet now.

The people from the time-shares are out in their canoes. They tip their caps as they pass personal watercraft, which are quietly executing decorative patterns in the water at a stately pace. Old people are driving the personal watercraft, the young people having learned the excitement of tree-spotting, a practice espoused by influential and aging rock singers.

Sailboards are back, and sailboats are on the increase. A new culture of slowness has captured the lake. While the proposed legislation to make napping mandatory failed, the practice has grown in popularity and has been featured on the cover of several magazines.

Waving from the docks and wearing their sunblock are people with the faces of Asia and Africa and Latin America, the second generation of visible minority cottagers, after the WASP monopoly was broken earlier in the century. Immigrants discovered the joys of the cottage, learned the strange customs of cottagers; at the same time, cottage country discovered the joys of diversity. New customs and games and food are enriching cottage life, and new music as well, although the antinoise covenants keep the volume down. Noise is the new smoking, it has been observed. (The previous new smoking was smoking.) Several abandoned golf courses have been turned into cricket pitches and soccer fields. Others have been given over to a popular new pursuit, silent nature walks. Dragon boat racing has become part of the August long weekend triathlon.

At the marina, the daily pickup of blue, black, green, red, orange, and grey boxes is under way, their contents proof of the commitment of cottagers to recycling. The parking lot is only half-full because the cottagers have taken advantage of the carpooling incentives. The highways are only half-full too.

The incentive plan to break up the large estates has worked well. There are more cottages but fewer lawns, and the boats are smaller, due to the effectiveness of the horsepower taxes. The new cottages are smaller and set back from the lake, much like the older cottages, which have survived as a result of other changes in taxation, designed to allow cottages to remain within families. The age of ostentation is over. Those who once owned cottages as status symbols got rid of them, having found them too much work. They decided they preferred to hang out in the city, going to festivals and enjoying the air conditioning. Their giant glass and steel palaces have been torn down, replaced with smaller buildings constructed of wood. The personal helicopter fad never got off the ground.

Once they learned that living at the cottage year-round was not the same as living in the suburbs with a lake nearby, the all-season cottagers adjusted quite nicely, and their year-round presence made for a powerful voting bloc that pushed lawmakers to make laws to help cottagers and preserve the lake. The more effective environmental regulations and the kinder tax laws are good examples of cottager power.

As a rule, the cottagers are happy. Noise is under control. People turn the searchlights out at night. The lake is clean. The water is cold but not too. The overcrowding that everyone feared has not happened. It is easier to get to the city and back. This is partly because there is less city to get back to. The city has emptied out a bit. More and more people are moving to smaller towns, where life is less hectic and where the cottage is closer. When they arrive at the cottage, they are in a more relaxed mood and are not so tense on the day they have to leave. As a consequence we see a decline in such Type A cottage behaviour as nail gunning and power birding.

Medical science has eliminated many of the major fevers, such as beaver and hay. The last bad back was recorded in 2037. The zebra mussel is gone and the pickerel is back. Raccoons have been happily relocated to Iran. The emergence of cheap and effective solar power has reduced reliance on gasoline. There is less of it in the lake and on it. The always imminent threat of power failures is less frightening. The emergence of truly biodegradable products has cut back on the volume of sudsy stuff leaking into the water.

There are fewer accidents on the water. More cottagers know first aid. More of them know how to drive a boat and what the rules are. Fewer of them drink and get into the boat. Midnight water-skiing has almost been eliminated.

Except for the crows that wake you up at seven in the morning, cottage life is almost perfect.

❋   ❋   ❋

All of this assumes, of course, that we are capable of solving such problems as overcrowding, overtaxation, pollution, highway gridlock, greed, and conspicuous consumption. And, of course, we are, aren't we? Didn't we put a man on the moon? On the other hand, didn't we put an amusement park on that farmland over there?

The chapters to follow give some indications of what the future may bring to the cottage, some nightmarish, some rather nice. They are provided for your amusement only; don't make any serious investments based on them.

In the end we can know only that the cottage will stride bravely into the future, to the extent that a cottage can actually stride. The future holds many challenges and probably some pretty lousy weather too, but, as we have seen, everything will be fine. We cottagers are people of goodwill, capable of doing the right thing, as long as we get plenty of rest.

The Cottage Wedding

"I Do [slap!]"

In the glowing world of Cottage Future, more weddings are performed at cottages than at churches. And you can understand why. Nothing is more perfect than a perfect cottage wedding. The sun shines, the lake glistens, the birds sing, all of nature forms a perfect backdrop for the happiness of the happy couple and their happy guests, nicely yet comfortably attired in casual but elegant clothes.

You read about such perfect cottage weddings all the time in magazines. The photos look terrific, and when you come right down to it, what could be nicer? The noise and the congestion and the humidity of the city are avoided. There is no hotel ballroom to hire, no expensive sit-down dinner. There are no limousines – well, hardly any; you can think of some people who might want one, even at a cottage. Mostly, everything is simple, yet beautiful and peaceful. The cottage means so much to the couple and their families – or at least to the one that owns it.

Now, it's true that the simplicity of the event can be overstated. There may be fewer contracts to sign, but that is only because much of what others do in the city the family is doing here. The family is not paying out so much money, perhaps, but they are doing a lot more work.

This is because certain things that are taken for granted in a city wedding reception cannot be taken for granted at the cottage. Among these are:

Chairs
Tables
Tablecloths
Dishes
Glasses
More glasses
Ice
Liquor, beer, and wine
Bartenders
Glasses
Waiters
People to carry stuff
People to set it up
Parking
Glasses
Bathrooms

Organizers of a cottage wedding learn certain things. The most important is that carrying is a fine art, exercised continually. Stairs and paths make it infinitely difficult. The difficulty is increased if boats are included, to be loaded into and lifted out of.

They learn that there is an infinite number of ways to arrange tables, and that there is an infinite number of views as to how that should be done.

They learn the importance of flashlights.

Organizers of cottage weddings learn that portable-toilet rental companies do not do islands. It is one thing, as they point out, to deliver an empty plastic toilet structure to an island. It is another to retrieve, the next day . . . well, you get the idea.

Remembering, always, that a cottage wedding is the most perfect event that could ever happen, here is a partial list of things that can go wrong:

Rain.

Wind.

Cold.

Mud.

The rented furniture arrives requiring some installation; certain screws and bolts, necessary to keep the tables from tipping over, are missing, and no replacement parts are available, all the screws and bolts in the boathouse having been taken to the city in mid-July for some reason no longer remembered. Family members are required to stand beside the wobbly tables and prop them up until such time as the guests are themselves wobbly and unlikely to notice.

Snow.

The boat runs out of gas.

Wedding website attacked by a virus.

Bride's teetotalling father puts back out resentfully carrying cases of wine up steep stairs to cottage.

Computer-savvy cousin in charge of sending out online maps momentarily forgets that north is up. Ceremony begins after forty-five-minute delay, during which some guests presume the bar is open.

A swarm of mosquitoes is anticipated. The bride smells of DEET. A swarm of mosquitoes attacks, causing the ceremony to be punctuated by the sound of slaps.

Mosquitoes drive the ceremony indoors, where it is just like any other wedding ceremony anywhere, except in a smaller room.

A small convention of personal watercraft users is held just offshore.

Retired sea captain engaged as minister breaks into giggles while reading the part of the service that invokes the spirit of the woodchuck, the loon, and the toad.

The wind blows the flowers off the makeshift trellis.

Just offshore, a nine-year-old falls off her water skis in the middle of the ceremony and is subjected to vigorous shouted suggestions from her father in the boat.

The wind blows the makeshift trellis over, causing a loud bang and the groom's nonteetotalling uncle to make a loud observation, momentarily forgetting his wedding vocabulary.

The groom has poison ivy and tries not to scratch during the ceremony.

The maid of honour's pollen allergy puts in its yearly appearance. She comes down the aisle with a bouquet of lilies in one hand and a box of Kleenex in the other, eventually abandoning the lilies.

Bride's sister says: "This isn't what happened in the magazine."

Bridal party members return from wedding photo session in the woods, covered in pine needles and sap.

Daylight portion of the reception marred by wasps, attracted to wineglasses.

Fourteen-year-old nephew enlisted as bartender attempts to make a tequila sunrise.

Dinner portion of the reception marred by complaints from overdressed members of groom's family, who object to eating standing up.

Someone left the cake out in the rain.

Dancing part of the reception marred by unfortunate accident involving bride's aunt, who, taking advantage of the only polka of the evening, sprains ankle on a tree root.

There is confusion, later in the evening, as to which is the tree selected for the use of the gentlemen.

A raccoon is spotted, mistaken for a bear, causing a search for bear spray that produces only hairspray. "I thought that's what you said," bride's uncle says, as the raccoon escapes into the forest.

The deejay, taking a break from his position as bartender, decides to crank it, causing formal, though anonymous, letters of complaint to the executive of the cottager's association and the adoption within the year of a Cottager's Code of Ethics.

Owing to shortage of flashlights, several gentlemen in search of tree crash into tents set up by younger guests.

Impromptu swimming features both fully clothed and insufficiently clothed guests. Photographs are instantly taken with the cellphone by computer-savvy cousin and posted on the wedding website.

Groom's nonteetotalling uncle mistakes pole of tent occupied by younger guests for gentlemen's tree.

New Heroes of Cottage Country

Mr. Fix-It

So here comes the new Mr. Fix-It, handyperson.com, a nerd with a four-stroke outboard, a laptop instead of a toolbox, not a saw or hammer in sight. You will really need him.

Generations ago, Mr. Fix-It used to be the uncle or cousin at your place who knew how to get the boat running, or the pump. Some days the water would run out and somebody would yell "Water's out!" That was the signal for every able-bodied man to pretend he couldn't, all of a sudden, hear, since starting the pump was a rather lengthy proposition, not to mention greasy.

At least, it was if you were being thorough about it. You had to make sure it was filled up, and the little oil places had oil in them. Less conscientious folks would assume that somebody else had taken care of the gas and oil and just pull the rope. Still, nobody wanted to do it. It was noisy and smelled like gasoline and oil, both of which you were likely to get all over you.

For a brief time in their lives, the teenaged boys didn't mind doing it. That's because starting the pump could be sold to them as a rite of passage, part of becoming a man. When they successfully started the pump, they would stride proudly up the path and say, as matter-of-factly as they could manage,

"Pump's going," whereupon everybody would congratulate them on being a man and give them a cookie, just in case they still liked that sort of thing.

The job of the pump was to lift water out of the lake and up the hill into a giant tank. The tank would provide all the water for washing and, in the best of circumstances, drinking. It might even provide water for flushing, if the appropriate plumbing arrangements had been made. The old, old pumps were giant turn-of-the-century (or turn of the *previous* century) contraptions, with large oil cups and giant flywheels and long leather belts. They were large enough to need their own houses. In the pumphouse, a large wooden crank was attached to the wheel, and after the oil cups were filled, the gasoline added, and the battery connected, the cranker would spin the wheel, making sure to keep his thumb out of the way, in case the wheel cranked back. There was a wonder to the machine and to the process, and it was not unusual for several people to work at it and several others to watch, so impressive was the whole thing.

When that pump wore out and parts were no longer available, it was replaced with something a tenth the size, just as noisy, but with a noise far less majestic. It sounded like a lawn-mower, or a chainsaw, or – much later – a personal watercraft, since the engines are all basically the same.

There was no wonder to this one. You filled it up, pulled the rope, adjusted the throttle, and hoped for the best. It was less fun to do, and fewer people wanted to do it, especially once the kids got on to the rite-of-manhood scam. But it was such a small and simple machine that it seemed wrong to call someone to fix it when it didn't work. Someone at the cottage always seemed to know how to do it. Usually it just involved pulling harder and cursing a bit.

Sometimes the pump would start but the water wouldn't run up the pipe to the tank. This meant, in the terminology of the time, that the pump "isn't pumping." The remedy for this was to grab the pipe that came out of the water and shake it.

Or grab the pipe that came out of the pump and shake it. This would get rid of air pockets or vacuums that formed and prevented the water from running up the hill. And even if it didn't really do that, it did seem to get the water running up the hill.

There was rarely a need to call Mr. Fix-It in those days. There was one on-site. Whatever was wrong with whatever gizmo, the on-site Mr. Fix-It would find the offending part, remove it, and go somewhere to get a new one.

For many cottagers, life is easier now. There is no water tank, but there is water. It comes when you turn on the tap. It may even be hot, if you want it that way. Water comes when you flush the toilet. It doesn't run out.

But there is still a pump. Now it turns itself on by electricity when a tap is opened or a toilet is flushed. This is a miracle and a mystery to many older cottagers. It is a mystery to them how to fix it if it stops working, which it can. The machinery is too complicated for the on-site Mr. Fix-It. Now a professional has to be called.

That would be the current Mr. Fix-It, handyperson.com's dad. He – usually a he – arrives in his metal boat, heads straight for the offending piece of machinery, and sets it right. Since the machinery is becoming more and more sophisticated, particularly in the sewage management department, Dad has become quite sophisticated himself. He knows what those coloured lights mean. He knows what reverse osmosis is and the ins and outs of filtration. But, because he is a lake person, he is also aware that the problem may have been caused by a chipmunk.

He can also fix the refrigerator and the dishwasher, should they be available and indisposed. You would never have seen his like in the cottage country of old. People did arrive in boats in those days, but they were delivering milk and ice, not fixing the things you kept the milk and ice in.

Whatever you think of the intrusion of modern gadgets into cottage life – the dishwashers and baseboard heaters, the microwaves and hot tubs – they contribute much to the local economy, because they break. An army of repairists and suppliers becomes necessary. Employment is created; money is poured into the local economy. With the money, houses are expanded and boats are purchased, which in turn will need repairs. Thus does the cottage economy sustain itself.

The connected cottage

Of course, handyperson.com's dad is far more sophisticated than his predecessor, but he won't be able to do all the things that will need to be done in the future. That is because refrigerators and hot tubs will not be enough for the future cottager. The future cottager needs, above all, to be connected.

This is why many of us have no interest in being future cottagers. We want to be ancient cottagers, who see the cottage as a place to escape the cares of modern life, instead of as a place to deal with the cares of modern life with a laptop on a screened verandah.

The connected cottager will want high-speed Internet, and someone will have to be there to sell it to him. The connected cottager's computer will break down, and cannot be fixed by shaking it. The connected cottager will have cellphone problems. His satellite TV set-up will have periods of inadequacy. Someone will have to hop into a state-of-the-art SUV or a new metal boat with four-stroke engine to deal with it.

And that will be handyperson.com. Some day, well into the future, they will tell stories about him, seated around the virtual campfire, the computer-generated crackle of pixelated flames punctuating the conversation. How he braved high winds and a heavy sea to eliminate a virus that was making text messaging impossible. How he, pursued by a bear, somehow managed to reconnect us to the Golf Channel. How he fixed the problem of nobody being able to get on the cottage website. How he got the central vacuum system working. How he Googled a perfect solution to the problem of the hornets around the barbecue. How he got the remote control working again to lower the dock into the water on a cold twenty-fourth of May weekend.

He's quite a guy, an essential element in Cottage Future. And he'll be there in a minute, as long as the system isn't down.

Fun for the Whole Family

The Cottage Website

Much as we may regret it, or much as we may not, the Internet comes to cottage country. As soon as you saw your first wedding website, you knew it was inevitable. You have a cottage and a family. Every family has a computer geek in it. Every family also has someone who thinks the wider world needs to know everything about it. The combination is irresistible. The result is the cottage website.

It comes as a blow to those who value privacy and to those who think that, as much fun as they are, family goings-on might be less than fascinating to the general public. But the cottage website is going to happen. People cruising through the Net in search of – well, you don't need to know what they are in search of; suffice it to say that it's a multifaceted world out there, and it takes all kinds – people cruising in search of something are going to stumble upon your cottage, or a virtual version of it. You don't want to give them the wrong idea. Hence, this guide to creating the perfect cottage website.

Begin with the name. It should be something catchy, beginning with www. If your cottage is called, perish the thought, Your Name's Slice of Heaven, then you will have a name (called a URL in computer-speak) like www.yournamessliceofheaven.com, except that some greedy little soul out there probably has already claimed it and will gladly sell it to you, along with a lot of other names that would be just right for you. This is why we need cottages, by the way, to get away from greedy little souls who want to sell our URLs back to us.

Your site will have many pages. The home page needs a title: "Welcome to Your Name's Slice of Heaven." Then a good picture. It could be a truly smashing photo of a sunset, which will inspire your cybervisitors to go immediately to another site. This may well be what you want. Or it could be a nice group shot of everybody in the family dressed in the Slice of Heaven T-shirts you had made up. This will also encourage Web visitors to go elsewhere. If you want them to stay, and heaven knows why you would, you should follow the principles of good journalism and run a picture of something gory. Any good cottage has many available – the time the tree fell on Aunt Gillian and the scab hadn't formed yet on her forehead, that accident with the fishing plug and Cecilia's thumb, the cousins all puffed up from the wasp stings. Such a photograph, as journalists know, will encourage casual visitors to stick around and go to other pages in hopes of finding out where the blood came from.

When they get there, of course, they will find the results of the last seven years' family croquet tournaments, Grandma's tips on making sushi, and a pictorial essay on the painting of the verandah, beginning with the scraping.

The front page of your site must have clickable links to other pages: Family Sporting Records, the Slice of Heaven Crossword (2 across: "Place where boats tie up" – four letters), Photo Gallery (many people holding fish, racquets, forks, hammers, and dogs), Cottage History, and, of course, the FAQs.

Maps are also good. A typical one will show the nearest large city – Toronto, Winnipeg, Montreal, Vancouver, for example – and an arrow pointed in the appropriate direction, along with the words *two hours*. Even if it's farther away than that, you don't want people to know, because it makes your cottage look low-rent. You also don't want to include any more detail. That could attract unwelcome guests. Welcome guests typically get their directions by telephone.

Many website visitors go straight to the Frequently Answered Questions, a must on any website, so these must be framed carefully. Note that there is a confusion between Frequently Answered Questions and Frequently Asked Questions. These are not the same, as any visitor to Question Period in the House of Commons can tell you. What you really want is to pose the questions that you wish were Frequently Asked, such as "How many years in a row have you won the croquet tournament?" and avoid the questions that are really frequently asked, such as "How much did this place cost you anyway?"

You are right to conclude that most websites feature Frequently Answered Questions that are not Frequently Asked. You should strive for this as well. Here are some good examples for your cottage website:

Q: What is the name of your lake?

A: Clear Lake.

Q: Are there any other lakes called Clear Lake?

A: Not so far as we know.

Q: Are there many different types of trees on your cottage property?

A: Yes. There are seven. Birch, poplar, oak, cedar, white pine, and two others that look something like that.

Q: Does everybody look forward to that first weekend at the cottage each summer?

A: You bet. Somehow summer isn't summer without the cottage, and winter isn't winter either, although we don't actually go there then so we're just guessing.

Q: How would you describe the call of the loon on Clear Lake?

A: We've given this a great deal of thought and settled on the word *haunting*.

The FAQs needn't stop there, of course, but that will give you an idea. It shouldn't be necessary to say so, but it bears repeating that there is no need, in the FAQs, to go into details on such topics as who thinks they deserve to get the place in the will, and which families do more work than others in keeping it up. Also, the various marriage breakdowns and their consequences need not be chronicled in detail.

For the same reason, it was probably a good idea to scrap the Cottage Diseases through the Years page.

Many online cottagers like the idea of posting various instructions – how to open the door, how to turn on the pump, where the fuses are, what to do if there's a dead raccoon in the pantry, and so on. Posting such instructions gives your website an impressive look, but you must remember that relatives standing at the cottage door trying to figure out how it opens are not likely to be online at that particular moment.

On the other hand, Uncle Matt may have his BlackBerry.

Finally, the matter of links must be addressed. It is the custom on personal websites to include links to other websites. The main purpose of this is to show the world the exciting range of interests the cyberoccupant possesses.

Links show the occupant's depth, as well as his sense of fun. They also serve the valuable purpose of getting the visitor the hell off the site and onto someone else's. This may be the reason links to pornography sites turn up in unexpected places. You probably don't want them on your website, and you also want to keep a close eye on your website manager, who is fifteen and may want to lead visitors off into exotic fields of hip-hop music and gothic gaming. On the other hand, linking to the official site of the rural municipality shows that you are a concerned citizen. Linking to the police and fire departments shows that you are safety-conscious. It is probably not a good idea to link with partisan political sites, and your sincere opposition to globalization is of little interest to those who landed on your site hoping to see something about fishing.

On the other hand, you want to show your fun side too. So, what the heck, go ahead and put in that link to the Official Woody Woodpecker site.

A Modest Proposal

The Royal Commission on Cottages was created in 2020, with the hope that it would have a vision. It was created to solve the Cottage Crisis, which was already well under way and had already brought about the downfall of one provincial government (over the Septic Tank Scandal of 2016). Large groups of Canadians were not speaking to one another, except on rare occasions. And on those rare occasions, they were speaking at the top of their voices.

"We live in an age of specialization," said the Royal Commission's terms of reference. "The cottage used to be a place where we went to get away from that. No matter what we did in our winter lives, no matter how technological or managerial or artistic our lives were, we would all become cottage workers – cleaners and sweepers and barbecuers and trimmers and hammerers and nailers, swatters of flies and mosquitoes and hunters after boards of a certain length.

"Within our group there might be subspecialties – people who were better at cooking or repairing or chopping or being dogs or little children. Each would have his or her role, but the overall function of being a cottage didn't vary much from one property to the next.

"That too has changed. Now we have cottages dedicated to being beautifully designed. We have cottages dedicated to partying and loud fun. We have cottages dedicated to being rustic and unspoiled, compared to cottages dedicated to having the latest gadgets. We have cottages for social animals and cottages for hermits.

"All of these contrasting places, dedicated to the celebration of differing pleasures, try to coexist on a single lake, and the results are not considered adequate by everybody. Everybody who can't find a place on the lake wants to be there. The people who have a place on the lake don't want anybody else to be there. The loud people annoy the quiet people. The new people annoy the old people. The newcomers feel patronized by the old-timers. The powerboaters terrify the canoeists. The canoeists get in the way of the powerboaters. Those who don't feel angry feel guilty. All of them feel that the lake isn't what they hoped it would be."

What to do? Since the cottage is a Canadian institution – not uniquely so, but it's as much ours as anyone else's, and more so than most – there had to be a Canadian solution. The obvious Canadian solution was to study the matter. To that end, the Royal Commission was established.

It travelled across the country, often by pontoon boat, and held hearings on docks and at yacht clubs. The commissioners – some old cottagers, a couple of developers, several token representatives of various demographics, three patronage appointments, and a retired judge – patiently listened to the complaints.

The commissioners heard various groups argue that nothing should be changed in cottage country and that the government must immediately introduce legislation to return cottage lakes to how they were one hundred years ago.

They heard old-timers arguing that newcomers were ruining everything. They heard newcomers arguing that the old-timers were profiteering like crazy on the sale of their properties. They heard entrepreneurs wanting to expand their lake activities and residents wanting a ban on those activities. They heard grandparents wanting the environment preserved for their grandchildren, and they heard grandchildren who thought their grandparents were nuts.

The commission heard from people who wanted to build spas, paintball establishments, places of worship, electronic bingo halls, monuments to 47 deserving groups who had suffered in one way or another, private clinics, a museum of moths, and a large specially ventilated facility where the people of an entire rural municipality could go to smoke.

The commission also heard from people who opposed each of these ideas.

After deliberating for a year, the commission released an interim report. It proposed the creation of a Permanent Cottage Authority, which would mediate disputes and enforce regulations. A respected former politician chosen from the usual talent pool would chair the Authority.

The Commission also raised the possibility of a typically Canadian remedy – zoning. Lakes would be zoned according to their use, the use to be decided in referenda among the cottagers. The Commission suggested, in its preliminary report, several possible broad designations for lakes – Quiet, Loud, Fast, and Slow. Residents would choose from among them. Quiet lakes would favour those who had no interest in electricity. Fast lakes would be for those who enjoyed personal watercraft and speedboats. Slow lakes would be for sailboats and canoes.

When the interim report became public, however, it became clear that the designations were not precise enough. Some cottagers wanted Slow *and* Quiet; others wanted Slow and Loud – for example, a musician who liked to practise the trombone in his canoe. Others favoured a Fast/Quiet hybrid, so that those returning from a speedy afternoon of personally watercrafting could take a nap.

Under vigorous cross-examination by lawyers for all the interested parties, expert witnesses from the universities testified, usually proposing refinements. For example, one sociologist suggested that each cottage day be broken into eight component parts, with a different designation for each. Thus, Fast times would be between noon and 4 p.m., Loud times would last from 6 until 10 p.m., the hours between 2 a.m. and 6 a.m. would be Slow/Quiet and 6 a.m. to 10 a.m. would be Fast/Quiet. The designations would switch from week to week, in a manner modelled after patterns of garbage pickup in the large cities.

Lawyers suggested variances – individual cottagers would, if authorized by the Permanent Cottage Authority, be allowed to nonconform on specified occasions. There were also statements made as to the constitutionality of the provisions relating to nap time.

When the final report of the Commission was released, the most hotly debated portion of its recommendations was that pertaining to the designation of lakes. Noisy residents of lakes zoned Napping and Jigsaw Puzzle resented having to move to a lake zoned Chainsaw and Barking Dog. In some cases, this would necessitate changing provinces, with all of the resultant tax implications. In one case, the zoning of a lake above the treeline as Leaf Blower and Hovercraft, a relocation of thousands of miles was required.

Some cottagers were pleased with the results, particularly those who would have their cottages at lakes reserved for napping and jigsaw puzzles, and hovercraft owners who would now be able to hover over their own lake with no concern over decibel levels.

But the satisfaction of some was outweighed by what many feared would be the large-scale breakup of families. As suggested in the draft legislation establishing the Permanent Cottage Authority, the PCA would have the power to banish certain family members from certain lakes if their activities did not meet the criteria. Critics of the legislation saw in it the possibility that children who enjoyed jigsaw puzzles would not be able to spend summers with their parents, if those parents happened to be at a lake zoned Personal Watercraft and Blaring Stereo.

Matters were not helped when the proposed head of the Permanent Cottage Authority said that she thought families were a bit overrated anyway, since children always went away eventually, and that the important thing was to get all cottagers on the same page. Newspaper editorialists took up the cudgels, arguing that our best cottagers would be migrating to the United States by the thousands to escape the legislation and Canada would be losing its most talented cottagers, not to mention hundreds of canoes, sailboats, and solar panels.

In response, cabinet ministers fanned out across the country, denying that the proposed head of the Permanent Cottage Authority was a patronage appointment. They further accused the critics of representing the money interests and being anti–Group of Seven.

Eventually, the issue was tested in the courts by a northern Ontario family who had lost two children as a result of a ruling by the Permanent Cottage Authority. Government lawyers, arguing on behalf of the authority, defended its decision to ship one child to Quebec and another to Montana because their interests (fishing and PlayStation, respectively) were not in conformity with the designation of the lake where the family cottage was located.

The government stated that it was necessary, under the North American Free Trade Agreement, to maintain a free flow of children across the border. This would justify the authority's decision to send a ten-year-old boy to a cottage in Montana rather than to his family's cottage near Sault Ste. Marie. Reversing the decision, it was argued, would anger the United States, which could still revive that softwood lumber thing.

The boy's parents argued that, while they would be delighted if the video games left the cottage, they were less delighted with the idea of the boy going with them.

Eventually, a landmark decision (the only kind ever made, if memory serves) was issued by the Supreme Court of Canada. The Permanent Cottage Authority, it ruled, violated the Charter of Rights and Freedoms, not to mention the Video Games Act of 2010.

After a public outcry, a Judicial Inquiry was set up to study the Royal Commission. Thus was the traditional cottage way of life saved, but only barely.

The Cottagers' Association
Faces the Future

Minutes of the Annual General Meeting, Crappie Lake Cottagers Association

1. The association agreed to renew the contract with the association lawyer.

2. The association agreed to renew the contract with the auditors.

3. The association agreed to renew the contract with the computer repairman, the Internet provider, and the Web designer.

4. Under correspondence, the Secretary read letters that contained the following complaints:

* The increase in business for on-site massage therapists and interior design advisers was causing congestion on the waterways.

* A cottager on the west side of the lake was allegedly operating his power weed mower after-hours, creating noise and making it difficult for neighbours to hear the music.

* The Crappie Lake Festival of Literature and Desserts sent a letter of appreciation, thanking the Association for its grant of fifty dollars and the use of the library meeting room.

It was hoped that next year's Festival would be bigger than ever due to the possibility of a collaboration with the annual Crappie Lake Fishing Classic and Poker Party.

5. After some discussion the Members agreed to open the bottled water contract to competitive bidding. Certain Members proposed that next year's bottled water be "fizzy"; however, a motion to that effect failed.

6. The Association heard a submission from Mr. Person, who said that he intended to run for the rural municipal council once he returned to the city. When asked why he would return to the city in order to run for a position in the rural municipality, Mr. Person replied that "this was the thing nowadays" – meaning that city people are demanding to be allowed to vote in rural municipality elections since they pay taxes here anyway and have a vital interest in RM matters, such as garbage pickup, dogs running loose, and the way the taxes have skyrocketed "out of control." Mr. Person added that he thinks association members who live in the city should also be allowed to vote in federal elections for candidates who represent constituencies in the cottage area. This would ensure that cottagers are represented in the federal Parliament. The Secretary asked, for clarification, whether dogs running loose was a federal or a provincial responsibility. It was agreed that the Secretary would ask for clarification from the Permanent Cottage Authority.

7. Under old business, the President reported that some progress had been made on the matters of raccoons and high-speed Internet. He made a humorous remark to the effect that he'd used high-speed Internet to look up raccoons. However, that was in the city, as high-speed Internet has not come to the RM, except in the library. A questioner from the floor asked if it was possible for the marina to provide hot spots for wireless users, and the President said he didn't know what any of that meant. He said he remembered a hot spot in town, but it was closed down fifteen years ago, after residents complained that it was too close to the elementary school. He added that the raccoons seemed to be less of a problem this year on his side of

the lake. The Vice-President said that the raccoons were still very active on his side of the lake and wondered if people from the President's side of the lake were bringing raccoons over in the middle of the night. A vigorous discussion followed.

8. It was pointed out that the Reeve of the Rural Municipality was in attendance, the Reeve having bought the property in the next bay from the marina. The Reeve said he was pleased to be a member of the association and that he had just paid his dues on the way in. The President asked if any Members had questions from the floor for the Reeve, and one Member asked how the progress was going on the helicopter pads. The Reeve replied that the RM was building helicopter pads as fast as it could and that cottagers should be patient. He reminded Association members that there once was a day when no cottagers owned helicopters.

9. A Member raised certain questions about the background music in the woods. He said that, while most Members enjoyed the music being broadcast out onto the lake, now that the samba music had been eliminated, parents with small children said that the music interfered with afternoon naps. They wondered if it would be possible to disconnect the speakers from trees on their property during the napping period. In discussion, a Member asked if it might not be possible to dispense with background music altogether. The President ruled this request out of order, saying that this country had been built on the principle of background music in as many places as possible and that he was offended by any suggestions to the contrary. The President did agree to set up a Music Committee of the Executive that would discuss the issue, but that there would be no reconsideration of the decision to allow the music in the first place, especially because of the importance of the commercials to the Association's budget.

10. The Environmental Committee reported that it was investigating complaints that garage doors were opening and closing mysteriously. A member asked if this had anything to do with "what is going on in Iraq." The President said that this was

a complicated matter and there was no precedent for action, since cottagers in earlier days managed to function without remote control garage door openers or, for that matter, garages.

11. The Nature Committee presented its report, the highlight of which was that the Chairperson's daughter saw a fish. That made four so far this summer, leading the Chairperson to express the belief that perhaps the fish were coming back. With respect to the young trees, the Chairperson said it was hoped that there would be more next year along Lakefront Road because no new cottagers are building helicopter pads this month.

12. Under new business, the Chairperson of the Water Depth Committee introduced a motion that the Association approach the Canadian government asking it to stop exporting Crappie Lake water to the United States, as Crappie Lake is two inches shallower this year. Speaking to the motion, the President replied that he was not sure that Crappie Lake water was really being exported to the United States, because how would it get there. He mentioned the absence of rainfall in July and August as a possible cause of the shallower water. The Chairperson of the Water Depth Committee said he didn't know about that but his boat had hit a rock that was never there before the Americans started buying our water. After discussion he agreed to defer the motion and see if anything happens the next time it rains.

13. Also under new business, a new company called Weddings On-Site was proposing to handle all cottage weddings on the lake next year, the number estimated at forty-six, perhaps forty-four if certain brides-to-be continued to spend so much time at the Tavern by the Dock.

The company would provide food and beverage services, portable toilets (islands excluded), video crews, disc jockeys, and ministers, if needed. In return for an exclusive licence to perform cottage weddings, Weddings On-Site would offer discounts of up to 15 per cent for Association members and a contribution to the Association.

The request was tabled after a lengthy discussion in which it was argued that cottage weddings were good for local business, although excessive rice throwing was having a harmful effect on the ecology. Furthermore, contestants in the Crappie Lake Bass and Karaoke Classic were concerned that the noise of wedding parties interfered with their concentration.

14. The Chairperson of the Heritage Committee recommended that the Association oppose the construction of more than one apartment building per island. She said it was true that most members had got used to the look of apartment buildings on islands, but thought that one was enough, particularly with the tall ones developers were building these days. Some developers were applying to knock down some of the older six-storey apartment buildings, which was clearly a heritage issue. It was agreed that the matter be referred to the Permanent Cottage Authority.

15. The President asked for a progress report on the drafting of the Cottagers' Code of Ethics. Mr. Bennett replied, on behalf of the Ethics Committee, that problems had arisen with regard to the issue of laundry being hung out on lines, causing an eyesore for boats passing by. As a result of this, it had been proposed that the Code of Ethics contain a provision that every cottage should have a washer and dryer; however, there was disagreement on this from the usual group of diehard, fanatical anti-electricity extremists. Otherwise, the drafting was going well, and the drafters were particularly pleased with the provisions relating to helicopter etiquette and the paving of forest paths.

16. Before adjournment, the President agreed to contact the police concerning the continuing problem of crime on Crappie Lake, in particular, the theft of insulated toilet seats.

The meeting adjourned at 8:45 p.m., in time for the boaters to return to their cottages while it was still light.

The Power Hammock

The Cottage Comes to the City

We are seeing a boom in cottaging, an explosion in real estate values and the beginnings of a trend to year-round cottaging, as baby boomers decide to retire and make their cottage a full-time residence. In addition, there is a steady and continual increase in the big-city technology and gadgetry available to cottagers. Cottage country, some of its inhabitants complain, is becoming too citified.

But the influence isn't all one-way. The city has a powerful influence, but cottage values are powerful too. As more and more people spend more and more time at their cottages, their approach to city living will change. Why shouldn't cottage values spread to the city, the same way city values are spreading into cottage country?

The impact of the cottage on the city means more than the seasonal lessening of the urban population that is felt so pleasantly by summer city dwellers – that sudden availability of seats on buses and on restaurant patios, the uncharacteristic ability to drive across the city in less than two hours, the quietness of the streets that makes the city so nice in the summer for those who can stand it.

Thoughtful urbanites are grateful to the cottage for such gifts, even if they never go near one. But the cottage's influence on the city goes beyond that. As the spread of the all-year cottage continues, city people are increasingly in contact with cottage people on a year-round basis. This turns some city people into cottage people and it stands to reason that some wilderness values will rub off and be taken back into town.

Then what? Productivity will suffer, of course. In the city, people will be having beers at odd hours and going on hikes, perhaps in malls, just when they are most needed at the office. They will be taking more sick leave, as the result of the health paranoia that affects many cottagers. "I can't come in today," they will say. "I've got swimmer's itch." Or it could be poison ivy. And don't even begin to think about how many days off imagined West Nile fever will produce.

There will be a rise in office napping. The workers will demand it, demand it without guilt, because the essence of a cottage mentality is an absence of guilt about napping. And the essence of cottage metabolism is the absolute need for a nap. The bosses will have to capitulate. Otherwise, the workers will fall asleep anyway.

The bosses will have to co-opt them. Could this lead to an infestation of hammocks in the workplace? It is too soon to tell, but there is certainly an opportunity for modern capitalism to spring into action here. A hammock is a perfectly saleable piece of office furniture if marketed in the proper way – to wit: the Power Hammock. As soon as power is associated with any product or activity, it becomes acceptable in the modern marketplace.

The Power Hammock will help drive the economy. Ironically, the frenzy caused by the production, purchase, and promotion of the Power Hammock could cause at least a temporary cessation of napping. There will simply be no time for it.

Eventually that will fade away and the Power Hammock will come to be a quietly accepted part of office life. Naps will occur. Unfortunately, because this is an office and because the concept of power is involved, naps will have to be somewhat different from the cottage variety. For one thing, it will not be acceptable behaviour to take a large Canadian novel with you into Napping Room #12 to fall asleep under. Furthermore, it will be necessary to put your name on the sign-up sheet, something unheard of at the cottage. Still, a nap is a nap, and it's better than none. It's always good to be refreshed for the afternoon commute.

Another welcome cottage-influenced diversion will be bird spotting. This enjoyable feature of cottage life rarely happens now in the modern office, but in the future it will be commonplace to see knots of workers at the office window commenting on what they see flying by. True, most of the time that will be a pigeon, but habits learned at the cottage die hard.

The rare enthusiast, a Power Birder, will have his bird book downloaded onto his BlackBerry, into which he enters each bird, perhaps differentiating between the pigeons on the basis of feather colour.

In the broadest sense, the influence of the cottage on city life will be felt in the area of productivity. It will decline. Cottage workers, those who toil on dock repairs and path clearing, are accustomed to a task lasting an entire day, or perhaps more than one, if it is the custom to nap instead of work in the afternoon. Any cottage veteran knows that an hour's task can be spread out into a day and, further, that far more workers will be assigned to that task than are necessary.

One person with a drill, a hammer, and the proper saw can do that dock job in an hour and a half. But four people can take at least a day, beginning with the two hours' worth of discussion and planning that precedes the actual measuring. That is followed by the assembling of materials, which involves also the finding of materials, which further involves consultation with cottage members who are not actually part of the work crew but who know where the materials might be and whether or not someone might have taken some of those materials back into the city last Sunday night by mistake.

All of this takes time, which nobody worries about too much because what else are you going to do before lunch.

As this cottage work ethic works its way back into the economic life of the city, the effects will be significant. Larger work teams will become necessary to do less work in more time. And while this could have a negative effect on productivity, as it is currently measured, it will have a positive impact on employment. Not only will more people be needed for each task, but even more people than that, since a number of them will be, at any given time, napping.

The combination of these factors with the economic stimulus of the Power Hammock will eliminate unemployment for all time, which you probably never thought about when you and those three other folks were trying to fix the dock.

Another positive impact on city life will be the gradual reduction in the speed of everything. Cottagers are not used to moving fast and don't care if they don't. That will make walking slower and traffic even slower than that. No harm can come of it, unless somebody cares. Fewer and fewer people will, since the traffic wasn't going anywhere anyway.

Other effects of the spread of cottage influence to the city include a sudden increase in the purchase of mystery books, a rash of diners showing up two hours later than they were supposed to, and the occasional appearance of sailboats in unexpected places. All of these are positive signs and should help to counter the occasional negative incident, such as the tendency of expatriate cottagers to want to cut the limbs off trees that don't belong to them because of compulsion to stockpile fireplace wood.

New Heroes of Cottage Country

Always at the Cottage

"You know what I miss most," Beth Walker said. She was sitting in her favourite wicker chair by the fireplace. The fire blazed. She had a drink and looked comfortable.

"What do you miss most?" Glenn asked, looking up from his *Golf Digest*.

"I don't miss anything," Beth said. "Isn't it weird not to miss anything?"

This was too deep for Glenn. He wanted to get back to thinking about this new way of cocking the wrists at the top of the backswing. He would try it next summer at Four Lakes when they got back to the cottage.

Except, and this always brought him up short, they *were* back at the cottage. Sitting right beside the double-glazed picture window, outside of which it was snowing. Inside, it was the same old cottage – the big wood coffee table some previous owner had made out of pine and varnished within an inch of its life, the old *Cottage Life*s and *Golf Digest*s strewn over it, along with pictures of last summer at the cottage and last winter at the cottage and that enlargement that they meant to get framed of last fall at the cottage.

Glenn picked it up and looked at it again – the two of them standing by the woodpile with the trees glowing around them. It was the answer to a question they had always asked: What would it be like to spend the fall here? The answer: It was pretty nice, once they got the new windows, the insulation, and the gas fireplace that made the woodpile more a decoration than a real woodpile.

That was too bad, not having the woodsmoke smell in the house. Still, it was nice not to have to go outside in the winter and get wood when they wanted to have a fire. When they were at the cottage next summer, he would have to think of doing something about that pile of wood. It probably was causing the siding to rot, leaning against the house like that.

Except that the siding wasn't wood. It was aluminum siding. And except that they already were at the cottage.

They were always at the cottage. It was what they had talked about for years – to be able to see the lake in the winter, the familiar trees now unfamiliar, covered with snow and winter birds; to watch spring arrive, see the trees begin to grow familiar again as the leaves appeared; to look for the first loon, the first beaver; above all, to catch the quiet, the stillness after everyone else had left, the lake with no boats, the opposite shore with no lights.

And now they had it. Actually, there were a few lights now on the opposite shore, but that didn't matter. There might be more in a year or so. Sometimes Glenn and Beth talked about that, but not for long, because they were living their dream and why spoil it by thinking negatively?

Thinking negatively would mean thinking about the entire shoreline lit up at night, the winter lake buzzing with snowmobiles, the sounds of laughter and amplified music carried on the clear winter air.

Beth would not allow Glenn to talk about it. Once, they heard what sounded like a string quartet coming from the next bay, and Glenn took a deep breath and was about to say something when Beth said, "What nice music," and that was the signal for Glenn not to say anything more and he didn't.

Now she looked into the gas fire and sighed contentedly and said, "It's perfect, isn't it?"

"Mmmm," Glenn said, and wondered if his backswing was too short.

"You know what I miss most?" Beth said.

Glenn looked up. "Didn't you just ask that?"

"I don't miss anything is what I said. Now I think what I miss is missing anything."

The backswing was going to have to wait. "What you're saying," Glenn said, "is that you miss missing something."

They had been married a long time. "I knew you'd understand," Beth said.

Glenn was sad that he understood. "You're saying that you don't like it here," he said.

"I didn't say that. I said I didn't miss anything."

"Then you said that you missed missing something."

"Yes."

"So what do you miss missing?"

Beth looked into the fire and tried to imagine smelling woodsmoke. "I miss missing the cottage," she said.

"You can't miss the cottage because you're here."

"That's right. And it's what I've always wanted."

"Me too," he said. "I like the quiet. I like the trees. I like the wind. I like the weather. I hated going back to the city. Now we don't have to. Isn't that great? You don't miss the city, do you?"

"No," Beth said. "I don't miss the city. What I miss is being in the city and looking forward to being at the cottage."

If Glenn had been thinking, he would have immediately proposed that they drive into the city, rent a hotel room, have a good meal and some hotel room sex, and then sit around missing the cottage. Then they could come back to it. And the thought did cross his mind, but he looked out the window and the snow and thought of the long drive to the city, remembered how they always hated that drive, how they would never drive up to the cottage in the wintertime because of how awful the drive was.

"We can't go back to the city," Glenn said. "Remember how much work it was to move up here full-time. Remember how much money we had to spend on this place, remember all that negotiation with our bosses, getting the computer stuff rigged up so we could work here. Remember how worried the kids were about us and how we had to talk them out of it. There's no going back now."

Beth shivered a bit. She reached over to the table beside her, picked up the remote control, and raised the level of the gas flames.

"I know there's no going back," she said. "But that's the other thing. I miss missing the city too. Remember how we'd spend a summer out here and when it was over we were sad to leave but always had fun when we got back, enjoying the novelty of hot water and lights that went on without lighting them, and the washing machine and even the TV and going to restaurants and movies."

"But we have all that now," Glenn said.

"That's the point," said Beth. "We have all that now. We don't get to miss it. And we don't get to miss the cottage because we're at it all the time."

"So what do you want?"

"I don't want anything. How could I want anything, if have everything? I've got high-speed Internet, three hundred channels off the satellite dish, electric heating, a dishwasher, washing machine, DVDs, CDs. Why would I want to go to the city?"

Glenn hadn't the faintest idea where this was heading, and he knew he wasn't going to like it when it got there.

"We're the envy of all our friends," he reminded Beth. "They all say they'd do just what we've done if they could afford it. They'd get a piece of property beside the lake, modernize it, insulate, and set up their work so they could work from the cottage. Then they'd live there all year-round."

"Right," Beth said. "Then they'd move in next door, and we'd never miss our friends either."

"You sound unhappy about that."

"I am. It's a terrible thing if you can't miss your friends."

Glenn decided he had to think. That meant taking his thumb out of the golf magazine, where it had been marking his place, waiting for his wife to return to her senses. She wasn't going to.

"Why don't we go somewhere else for a while?" he suggested.

"Like where?"

"I don't know. Go south, someplace warm, lie on the beach, drink things with umbrellas in them, eat at the hotel restaurant. Or we can go to New York, catch a couple of shows, go back to the Guggenheim, hit the stores."

He looked at his wife, who was gazing out the window at the snow.

"Or," he continued, "we could go out west, visit your folks, maybe see the Canucks play, walk in the rain. Or we could just go into the city for awhile, see our friends, check in at the office, show the flag, take the kids out for dinner."

She was still gazing.

"What about," Glenn said, "we go on a big cruise. Hop on an ocean liner, go across the Pacific, get off at Fiji or the Great Barrier Reef, do some snorkelling, eat a lot of fish, get a great big tan, then sail back and hang out by the pool all the way, spend lots of time on the dance floor, and read great books in our deck chairs while the steward brings us tea."

"What, and leave this?"